MORE JURY TRIALS
in the Classroom

MORE JURY TRIALS
in the Classroom

Betty M. See
Legal Advisor: Diane Elizabeth See
Illustrated by David Parker

PRUFROCK PRESS INC.
Waco, Texas

Prufrock Press Inc.
P.O. Box 8813
Waco, TX 76714-8813
Phone: (800) 998-2208
Fax: (800) 240-0333
www.prufrock.com

Contents

Introduction vii

Part I: Background Information

Chapter 1
Mock Trials as a Teaching Tool 3

Chapter 2
Court Systems of the United States 7

Part II: Structuring the Mock Trial

Chapter 3
Planning Your Mock Trial 15

Chapter 4
Conducting a Mock Trial 23

Part III: The Trials

Chapter 5
Criminal Trials 37

The State v. Gerry Rabbitt and Lu Fox 39

United States v. Susan B. Anthony 63

Chapter 6
Civil Trials 89

Goldie Locks v. Jo Deer, Owner and Editor
of the Gumperville Gazette 91

Squanto Jones v. Myles Standish 113

Appendix: Glossary of Legal Terms 137

About the Author 139

Introduction

When *Jury Trials in the Classroom* was first published, I had no idea that it would be received as well as it was. In hindsight, I should not have been surprised. Looking back on my experiences with mock trials during my years teaching gifted students in grades 5–8, I knew that these trials were eagerly anticipated not only by my students, but by teachers and students in the general school population. These students participated by not only attending the trials, but, in some cases, serving as jurors. It was always interesting to note how carefully the audience and jury listened, observed, and formed opinions using the facts given.

When I first conducted mock trials in the classroom, I used materials supplied by the local bar association. Students were divided into two teams, one representing the prosecution or plaintiff and the other representing the defense.

The trials were an immediate success, but I soon found that the trials supplied by the bar association were not always suitable in content and theme for middle school students. The solution was to write original trials. Thus began the process that resulted in the original *Jury Trials in the Classroom*.

When I was approached to do a sequel to the first book, I knew the biggest problem would be to create new scenarios for both criminal and civil trials. I asked family and friends for possible suggestions. Coming up with the principal characters for the trials was challenging. Creating something interesting, at times humorous and doable, was daunting. The trials are written at different levels so that there are choices for students in grades 4 to 6 and for students in grades 7 and up.

The first criminal trial is *State v. Gerry Rabbitt and Lu Fox*. The main characters in this trial have been charged with illegal betting and influencing the outcome of a race between Gerry Rabbitt and Jamie Tortoise. The more difficult of the two criminal trials is *United States of America v. Susan B. Anthony.* Susan B. Anthony and several other women were actually brought to trial for illegal voting in November 1872. Anthony was found guilty in what many deemed an unfair trial in which the presiding Judge Ward Hunt advised the jury to deliver a guilty verdict. The trial presented here is the result of a *hypothetical appeal.* At the time of the trial, no appeal was allowed. This trial provides the students with a wonderful opportunity to examine the U.S. Constitution and interpretations of it.

The first civil trial is *Goldie Locks v. the* Gumperville Gazette. Ms. Locks, who is a real estate agent, is suing the local newspaper because of a story they had printed on the front page of the paper that falsely accused her of trespassing. She claims it has damaged her reputation and cost her in real estate commissions. The other civil trial, *Squanto Jones v. Myles Standish,* is for older students. Set in present day New England, Squanto Jones runs a restaurant called Wampanoags' Restaurant. Several years ago, Myles Standish and a group of immigrants from England settled in the area. Because the newcomers did not know the area or how to raise crops and live off the land, Squanto Jones and members of his tribe helped them, showing them how to survive and even prepare native foods. The English settlers quickly became independent. In a few years, they opened their own restaurant called Pilgrim's Fare in direct competition with Wampanoags' Restaurant. Most of the items on the menu were thinly disguised copies of those served at Wampanoags' Restaurant. As a result, Squanto Jones' restaurant lost a great deal of business. He is suing Standish, charging that the stolen recipes could be regarded as trade secrets.

As with the original *Jury Trials in the Classroom,* my daughter, Diane See, a criminal defense attorney, has lent her expertise. She has served as a reference source and has given advice on the legal aspects of each case that add to its validity.

Jury Trials and the Middle School Curriculum

Simulation activities have always proved to be very popular with both students and teachers. When a student is involved on many levels, it makes for a memorable learning experience. Mock trials present students with situations (sometimes based on fictional characters and sometimes based on real-life events) where the problem is resolved in a courtroom setting. The students take on the roles of attorneys, defendants, plaintiffs, witnesses, and jurors. They prepare arguments to support each side and in the end resolve the issue by a vote of the jury.

These activities accomplish several objectives at the same time. Mock jury trials provide opportunities for students to:

- understand the judicial system,
- work cooperatively,
- write persuasive statements,
- read analytically,
- integrate information from several sources,
- think evaluatively and render judgments, and
- prepare and deliver oral presentations.

Part I:
Background
Information

CHAPTER 1

Mock Trials as a Teaching Tool

From the time of the ancient Greeks to modern TV trials, man has sought to bring to justice those individuals or groups who are believed to have broken society's rules. They may have been charged with committing a crime against laws written by governing bodies or they may have been perceived as violating the civil rights of others.

Through the media and personal experiences, today's students are exposed to the judicial process in many ways. The challenge we face as teachers is to help our pupils understand the complexities of our legal system.

When teaching the three branches of the United States government—executive, legislative, and judicial—students usually have practical examples in the classroom of the executive and legislative levels. Classroom elections and student government meetings offer the opportunity for them to experience how these branches work. Indeed, the administration and faculty can act as examples of the executive branch and decision making by students in the classroom can act as a sort of legislative activity.

Sorely lacking in most curricula is an in-depth study of our judicial system. Unfortunately, the perception of the mechanics of how our jury system works is often gained from fictional trials in movies or TV where justice triumphs through some miraculous last-minute discovery. The planning, hard work, and knowledge necessary to bring a case to trial are glossed over due to time constraints.

As teachers, we can read about the trial process or we can allow our students to experience the challenges each side faces in bringing a trial to court. When working with the evidence and statements of witnesses, students use higher thinking skills to plan their strategies and present the best possible case for their side. The importance of inferential reading skills becomes readily evident.

Cooperative learning takes place naturally. Teamwork, which is usually associated with the athletic field, becomes an absolute necessity if a side is to present its case most effectively. As students plan their mock trials, they learn how to evaluate evidence and formulate questions so that their case is presented in the best possible light.

While a jury verdict in their favor might seem to indicate a win for a team, students soon realize that in some instances, no matter how well lawyers or witnesses have planned their strategy, a decision in their favor is not likely.

It must be emphasized that lawyers spend 3 years in law school and have experience in mock trials (sometimes known as moot court) before entering the real world of a trial attorney. Indeed, it may be some time before he or she is actually the lead trial attorney for a case. The fact that an individual's freedom or civil rights are at stake demands that attorneys have experience in hypothetical cases and in assisting other attorneys before they handle the actual responsibility of serving as lead attorney.

We cannot expect students to perform as professional attorneys with the amount of training they receive in a classroom setting. We can, however, make them aware of what is involved in the judicial process to help them understand that many hours of preparation are involved before a trial actually reaches the courtroom.

As an example, my class took a field trip to the county courthouse. We had hoped to see a trial in session. When we entered the courtroom, the only individuals present were the judge, the opposing attorneys, and one witness. The witness was an elderly woman. She was there to determine if she had a hearing deficiency sufficient enough to require an interpreter. After she left, we spent the rest of our time there (about an hour) listening to the judge and the attorneys formulate questions that were to be presented to prospective jurors. This was a criminal trial in which the defendants were charged with stealing possessions from the elderly woman's apartment under the guise of helping her.

The students were disappointed that they had not seen the actual trial, but they saw something equally as important—some of the painstaking hours of preparation that occur before the trial. They saw how the wording of a question could favor one side over another. When we returned to class to prepare for our trial, they were much more aware of the phrasing of their questions.

By learning how our court system works, students will have a better understanding of major trials that have proved sensational and judicial decisions that have changed our every day lives. You might want to review some of the specifics of the following trials with your students.

- The Salem Witchcraft trials, which occurred from June to September of 1692, were the cause of death by hanging of 19 men and women.

- In the famous Scopes trial in the summer of 1925, John T. Scopes, a high school teacher, was charged with violating Tennessee law by teaching evolution.
- Another spectacular trial was the Lizzie Borden trial in Fall River, MA, in 1892. Miss Borden was acquitted of murdering her parents with an axe.
- A sports scandal was the focus of the infamous trial of eight Chicago White Sox players who were charged with "throwing" the 1919 World Series. It was widely referred to as "the Black Sox scandal." Supposedly prompted by the stinginess of White Sox owner Charles Comiskey, the players decided to get even. The jury acquitted them, but Baseball Commissioner Kenesaw Mountain Landis banned the eight players from ever playing baseball again.
- In the Lindbergh kidnapping trial, Bruno Hauptmann was charged with the murder of the Charles Lindberghs' baby son. Hauptmann was convicted and later executed.
- In 1997, many people were killed in the bombing of the Alfred P. Murrah Federal Building in Oklahoma City, OK. Timothy McVeigh was charged, convicted of the crime, and later executed.

Decisions handed down by the U.S. Supreme Court have played a major role in changing our society. Students also will benefit by learning about some of the trials that have been considered by the Supreme Court, including those on the following list.
- The Dred Scott decision in 1857 caused a major setback for slaves seeking their freedom. Scott, who lived in the Minnesota Territory, sued for his freedom based on the Missouri Compromise of 1820, which prohibited slavery in federal territories. The Supreme Court declared the already-repealed Compromise unconstitutional because it deprived a person of his property—a slave—without due process of law. It further stated that Black citizens descended from slaves had no rights as American citizens. Fortunately, this decision was invalidated by the 14th Amendment to the Constitution in 1868.
- In 1896, the U.S. Supreme Court issued a ruling in *Plessy v. Ferguson,* declaring that restricting the use by Blacks of public schools and public accommodations such as hotels, restaurants, and transportation facilities was legal and could continue. It was not until the 1950s that the Civil Rights Movement forced a change.
- In 1954, *Brown v. Board of Education of Topeka,* a seminal U.S. Supreme Court decision struck a major blow for school desegregation. The practice of having separate schools for Black and White children

was deemed inherently unequal, and public schools in America were required to admit students of all races. The unanimous Supreme Court decision paved the way for the Civil Rights Movement of the 1950s and 1960s to abolish segregation of Black and White American citizens.

• Undoubtedly, on TV shows or in movies, students have seen an individual being read his rights to remain silent and have an attorney present when arrested. The U.S. Supreme Court decision in *Miranda v. Arizona*, handed down in 1966, was responsible for this milestone.

CHAPTER 2

Court Systems
of the United States

One of the chief purposes of government, according to the U.S. Constitution, is to ensure domestic tranquility. The primary function of every court system is to keep such promises of peace and order. The courts, which are part of the judicial system, are the branch of the government that makes decisions about problems in civil and criminal law. Were it not for these courts, an atmosphere of violence and anarchy might prevail.

The United States' court system is one of the most complex in the world. Each state has a supreme court, courts of appeal, and courts of lower jurisdiction that handle minor civil and criminal offenses. The highest court in the land is, of course, the U.S. Supreme Court. Figure 1 gives a general idea of how our nation's court system is structured.

State Courts

Trial Courts

Also known as "trials of first instance," state trial courts deal with parties in conflict, hear witnesses, review evidence and facts, and reach a decision or verdict. The courts may further be divided into two areas—criminal and civil.

Criminal courts deal with individuals accused of a crime. The trial may be heard before a jury or the defendant may elect to have only a judge decide the verdict. In some states, the prosecution also has to concur with the defense to a

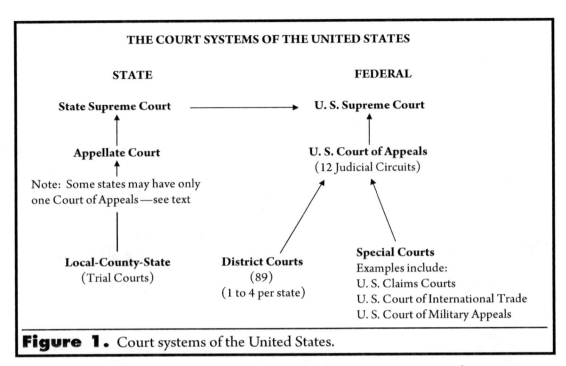

THE COURT SYSTEMS OF THE UNITED STATES

STATE   FEDERAL

State Supreme Court ————————▶ U. S. Supreme Court

Appellate Court   U. S. Court of Appeals
                                         (12 Judicial Circuits)
Note: Some states may have only
one Court of Appeals—see text

Local-County-State   District Courts   Special Courts
(Trial Courts)   (89)   Examples include:
                            (1 to 4 per state)   U. S. Claims Courts
                                                    U. S. Court of International Trade
                                                    U. S. Court of Military Appeals

Figure 1. Court systems of the United States.

bench trial (where the judge is the trier of fact) in lieu of a jury trial (where the jurors are the triers of fact). If the defendant is judged guilty, the punishment will vary depending on the severity of the crime and other factors, such as prior criminal record.

Civil courts deal with private problems between individuals or corporations. The public is not involved in civil actions and the state does not prosecute as they do in criminal cases. The object of a civil case in which the defendant is judged to be wrong is to attempt to restore the situation to what it might have been had no legal wrong been committed. In many instances, the defendant may have to pay money to the wronged party. These are called *compensatory damages. Punitive damages* are sometimes awarded against a defendant to punish him or her and to let the community become aware that such behavior will not be tolerated.

The court systems governing trial courts may vary widely from place to place. Major population centers may have courts of general jurisdiction, but to expedite matters, courts may be organized into special branches such as criminal, civil, traffic, and juvenile courts. In many areas, these courts are known as *inferior courts.* They may handle minor civil and criminal cases (such as misdemeanors and minor felonies). They may also handle preliminary parts of more serious criminal cases such as setting bail, advising the accused of his rights, appointing defense counsel, and deciding whether evidence justifies holding a defendant for a trial in a higher or *superior court.*

Example, State Trial Courts: Joshua Bartholomew has been arrested in Midville. He is accused of armed robbery of a Midville convenience store. After reviewing the evidence, the municipal judge has set bail and Mr. Bartholomew is sent to the local jail until bond can be posted. Mr. Bartholomew has retained the services of a local attorney (had he been unable to do so because of insufficient financial resources, a court-appointed attorney would have been named). Because of the seriousness of the charges against the defendant, the trial is transferred to a higher or superior court.

Appellate Courts/Supreme Courts

The courts mentioned prior to this are trial courts or courts of first instance. *Appellate courts* handle cases in which the fairness of the lower court's decision is in question. Most states name their highest court Supreme Court, New York being a notable exception, calling its highest court the Court of Appeals and using the designation Supreme Court for lower courts. Some states do not have intermediate appellate courts. These higher courts are usually presided over by several judges whereas trial courts only have one judge. The higher the court, the greater the force of its decision. The decision of a court is binding on lower courts within its jurisdiction, meaning that lower courts facing similar issues must follow the rules previously laid down by the higher courts.

If a party involved in a trial in a lower court feels that the trial ruling is wrong, the ruling may be appealed. An exception to this would be in the case of an acquittal of a defendant accused of a crime. If this individual was found not guilty, the state may not appeal the verdict nor may the defendant be placed in double jeopardy and tried again for the crime.

Example, State Appellate or Supreme Courts: In our case, Joshua Bartholomew, the defendant who was charged with armed robbery, has been found guilty by the jury hearing the trial. The judge has sentenced him to the state penitentiary. Mr. Bartholomew's attorney is appealing the verdict on the grounds that the judge made errors during the trial by not allowing several pieces of evidence to be introduced that would have been favorable to the defendant. The appellate court will review the case and if they feel that this evidence should have been admitted, and that the verdict could have been affected by the omission of the evidence, the court will probably order that the case be retried. The original judge may preside at the retrial unless some particular bias was shown or unless the judge is no longer assigned to that court.

Federal Courts

In accordance with Article III of the Constitution, federal constitutional courts were created. These include the district, circuit, and supreme courts of our federal government.

Special Courts

Article III vested in Congress the power to create special courts. Examples of this type of court include:

- *The U.S. Claims Court* has jurisdiction over monetary claims against the United States based on the Constitution or acts of Congress.
- *The U.S. Court of International Trade* has jurisdiction over civil actions against the U.S. involving federal laws governing imports.
- *The U.S. Court of Military Appeals* reviews court martial convictions for all of the armed services. This court is subject to review by the U.S. Supreme Court only in a limited number of cases.

District Courts

These are trial courts of general federal jurisdiction. They hear all matters that relate to federal laws and some cases that involve citizens of different states. There are 89 courts, including at least one in each state and the District of Columbia. Larger states such as California and New York have four. Usually one judge presides, but in some cases it is required that three judges are called together to make up the court.

U.S. Court of Appeals

These courts were created to relieve the U.S. Supreme Court of having to reconsider all trials originally decided by federal courts. Decisions of these courts are final except when law provides for direct review by the Supreme Court. There are 12 judicial circuits that compose the court of appeals system and each of the 50 states and the District of Columbia is assigned to one of them.

U.S. Supreme Court

The highest court in the land is composed of nine Supreme Court justices, one of whom is named the Chief Justice. In both civil and criminal law, the United States Supreme Court is the ultimate court of appeal. All other remedies must be exhausted before petitioning the Court for appeal or review of a lower court decision. Cases originating in state courts can be appealed to the Court directly from state supreme courts. Cases originating in federal court must go through the U.S. District Court and U.S. Court of Appeals first. The Court itself decides whether to hear a case or let a decision stand. In all cases, the Court will decline to review decisions lacking a substantial federal issue.

Example, U.S. Supreme Court: A case that reached the U.S. Supreme Court was *Griffin v. California* (1965). Griffin was convicted of murder in the first degree after a jury trial in a California court. He did not testify at the trial. The Fifth Amendment of the U.S. Constitution states that no person "shall be compelled in any criminal case to be a witness against himself." The prosecutor made much of the failure of the defendant to testify, inferring that this proved his guilt. The trial court judge instructed the jury that it was the defendant's constitutional right not to testify; however, he went on to state that the jury may take this failure to testify into consideration. The defendant was found guilty and sentenced to death. The California Supreme Court upheld the conviction. Because a matter involving the U.S. Constitution was involved, the case was sent to the U.S. Supreme Court.

The Supreme Court reversed the lower court ruling. Justice William Douglas wrote the opinion for the Court stating, "What the jury may infer, given no help from the court is one thing. What it may infer when the court solemnizes the silence of the accused into evidence against him is quite another . . . We take that in its literal sense and hold that the Fifth Amendment . . . forbids either comment by the prosecution on the accused's silence or instructions by the court that such silence is evidence of guilt."

As a result of the Supreme Court ruling, the case was reversed and remanded for a new trial with the proper instructions read to the jury.

Although the previous descriptions of our country's legal system are simplified, they should serve as a basic introduction to its structure. *Remember that the structure of the court system may vary from state to state and the names of courts on similar levels may also be different.* Check to see how your state judicial system may vary from what is presented here. Make these adjustments in your presentation to your class.

Part II: Structuring the Mock Trial

CHAPTER 3

Planning Your Mock Trial

Conducting a mock trial in your classroom can be a rewarding activity and a rich educational experience for everyone involved. Today's children have been exposed to trials in the news, in movies, on TV, and in the world around them. Explaining to them how our legal system works and having them participate in a trial simulation will help them better understand the intricacies of our court system. The four mock trials presented here have been designed for use with students in fifth through eighth grades. They have been written following the successful format used in the original *Jury Trials in the Classroom*.

Principal Participants

Attorneys (4–6)

You will need a minimum of two attorneys for each side. Ideally, two to three per side works best. Delivering opening and closing statements and conducting direct and cross-examinations can be overwhelming for one student. In addition, should a student be absent, other attorneys can cover his or her duties.

Witnesses (6–8)

Three to four witnesses for each side work best. Less than three will not fully develop the case. More than four will cause the activity to drag out too long. It is important that each student takes on the identity of the witness he or she portrays. How would this individual think and speak? What background would such a person have? By becoming the witness, the student will be much better able to handle cross-examination questions. All witnesses participate in the formulation of direct examination questions and also can assist the attorneys in cross-examination ideas for the opposition. It also is important to try to anticipate what each witness might be asked on cross-examination.

Other Participants

Not every student is going to want to be in the limelight for your mock trial; however, those who are not attorneys or witnesses should be actively involved in trial preparation. They should have access to trial materials and can participate in discussions regarding questions and strategies. They are part of the team. They may be called upon to do research and prepare evidence. (You may choose specific students as research assistants or select them as the need arises.) These students may also assume the roles of the following individuals who play an important role in bringing a case to trial.

Bailiff

This individual may see to it that the courtroom is set up properly and guide jurors and those watching the trial to their seats.

Court Reporter

Because your students will not have the skills of a professional in this area, an audiotape recorder may serve as the official transcript of the trial. One student should be in charge of the recorder and preparing the final tape of the transcript.

TV Camera Operators (2–3)

Because TV cameras are now allowed in many courtrooms (with some dispensing of the court reporter and just videotaping the proceedings), a video recording can be made of the proceedings. The camera should be in a fixed position in a place that will permit the audience to view the judge, attorneys, and the witnesses. Care should be taken that microphones pick up the voices of the trial participants only.

Research Assistants (2–4)

In some cases, research may be necessary to get more information about facts given in affidavits. For example, if a witness qualifies as an expert, try to find out more information about his or her field.

These students may also be called on to prepare charts, diagrams, and floor plans or site plans of crime scenes. We have not included these items in this book because of size limitations. In addition, the strategies used would determine if such items are applicable to a particular trial. By letting the students decide which items to use as evidence, the mock trial experience is closer to a real-life situation. To be effective, any visual aids must be large enough for the jury to observe in the courtroom setting.

Because it is not advisable or permissible to have actual weapons (guns, knives, etc.) in school, your research assistants may be called upon to make replicas of these items. Heavyweight cardboard or foam board may be used to make satisfactory copies.

Jurors (Eight—Six jurors and two alternates.)

When choosing jurors, it is important to have members who have had as little access to trial information as possible. We usually have used students from another class to serve in this capacity. You may ask the teacher to select students for the jury or you may draw names. In any case, their identities are not divulged until immediately before the trial. Siblings or relatives of trial participants are automatically excluded because they may be biased.

When the jury is impaneled, the two alternates sit with the six jurors to hear the trial. When the jurors leave to deliberate, the two alternates are excused. It should be explained to the students that the alternates are necessary in case one of the six jurors cannot remain for the whole trial. (It is advisable not to tell the jurors which students are the designated alternates until the judge is ready to send the jury to deliberate. If all of the students seated in the jury box are led to believe that they are the actual jurors who will be deliberating, the theory is that they will pay closer attention to the trial because they will be charged with rendering a verdict.) The alternates should be designated No. 1 and No. 2 when they are selected and serve in that order if necessary. Prior to the trial, be sure to have an area reserved where the jury can deliberate in privacy.

Audience

The best audience is a class that is not familiar with the trial. Although an audience is not essential, it serves to enlarge the group of students who learn about the judicial system. On the day before, this class should be briefed on the basic facts of the trial they will see and courtroom procedure. Table 1 includes an example of guidelines that can be used to brief the other class.

Preparation Hints for a More Effective Trial

When preparing for your mock trial, the two sides should work independently. Although each witness knows the questions that will be asked of him or her on direct examination, as in real trials, they will not know what will be asked on cross-examination. It is, therefore, very important that each attorney and witness try to anticipate what questions might be asked on cross examination. Each side should also be aware that any information discussed in strategy sessions should be treated confidentially. To ensure that trial materials are not circulated, I do not allow students to take them out of the classroom. If the opposition knows what will happen, the element of surprise will be lost.

As an example, my class had a mock trial in which a burglar was identified by someone who saw him through a curtained window. The defendant's attorney stated that if the window had a curtain, identification could not be made. The individual who saw the perpetrator was a prosecution witness. He said he had a clear view of the robber's face because the curtain was café style and only came halfway up the window. The defense was clearly at a disadvantage. They had made no attempt to identify the curtain style.

In working with the witness's affidavits, look for minor details that can work to your advantage. Each case has been designed to have weaknesses for both sides.

Table 1
Mock Trial Audience Information

Teachers using another class to serve as the audience and/or jury for the mock trial should brief the other students before the trial begins. Make sure to tell students that the opposing sides in the trial have not met prior to the court appearance. They have prepared questions for their own witnesses but do not know what may be asked of their witnesses on cross-examination. Emphasize that the mock trial is not a play—neither side knows what the opposition has prepared in direct or cross-examination questions. The following information is also applicable when briefing students.

Statement of Facts

Tell the students the basic facts of the trial. Be sure to give no more information than is contained in the Statement of Facts. Do not give names of students who will be the attorneys or will take on the personas of the witnesses.

Jury Selection

Inform the students that members of this class will be chosen to serve on the jury; however, they will not know who has been chosen until immediately before the trial. There will be six jurors and two alternates. The alternates will sit with the rest of the jury in the jury box. If any of the original six jurors cannot be available for deliberation, one of the alternates will be called on as a replacement. When deliberation begins, the alternates are excused. You may have the first of the six jurors called act as the jury foreperson and serve as spokesman for the group or you may have the jurors choose their own foreperson, as is done in real life.

Courtroom Procedure

The students should be aware that this trial will follow the format of an actual trial and the following courtroom rules will be followed:

1. All participants and observers rise when the judge enters the courtroom.
2. The judge instructs the jury about the trial they are about to hear.
3. Opening statements will be given by attorneys for the prosecution or plaintiff and for the defense.
4. Attorney(s) for the prosecution/plaintiff will begin direct questioning of witnesses for their side. After each witness is questioned, attorney(s) for the defense may cross-examine.

Table 1, continued

5. Attorney(s) for the defense will begin direct questioning of witnesses for the defense. After each witness is questioned, attorney(s) for the prosecution/plaintiff may cross-examine.

6. After each side has completed questioning, attorneys for each side will give summations or closing arguments.

7. The jury will deliberate. After they have reached a verdict, they will be led back into the courtroom by the bailiff. The judge will ask if they have reached a verdict, and the foreperson will answer, "We have, your honor." In the event that the jury could not reach a verdict, the foreperson will answer, "We have not been able to reach a verdict, your honor." This is a hung jury. The judge may ask to see the verdict in writing or may ask the foreperson to state the jury's decision. At this point, the judge may render a decision on what action will be taken next.

   a. In a criminal trial, the jury must reach a *unanimous decision* that will determine the guilt or innocence of the defendant. If there is a reasonable doubt of guilt, the defendant must be judged not guilty.

   b. In a civil trial, a unanimous decision is not required. In most states, four or five of the six jurors must agree in whose favor the evidence weighs most heavily. Check your local courts to find out what procedure they follow. The decision is based on a *preponderance of the evidence.*

In preparing for your mock trial, you'll want to read over the sections that follow, as well as consult the timetable given in Table 2. The timetable will help you allot sufficient time for your students to create an interesting, exciting, and enjoyable trial simulation.

Check the Facts

Opening statements may be written beforehand and read to the jury. Attorneys may also have direct examination questions in hand while questioning their witnesses. Although cross-examination questions and closing statements also may be prepared before the trial, attorneys should be aware of information given in court that might lead to additional cross-examination questions and might prompt changes and additions in the closing statements.

Table 2.
Time Allotments for Planning Your Mock Trial

No. of Sessions (45 min. each)	Concepts
1	Review structure of legal system Differentiate between civil and criminal trials Identify participants in a trial and the role each plays
1 to 2	Explain courtroom procedures Introduce simplified rules of evidence Distinguish between questions used in direct examination and cross-examination
1 to 2	Read Statement of Facts and affidavits for specific case to be used for your mock trial
2	Assign mock trial roles to individual students Prepare direct examination questions Prepare exhibits (charts, reports, letters) that might be necessary for trial
2	Prepare cross-examination questions for opposition Try to anticipate which questions opposition may ask in cross-examination Continue preparation of exhibits
1	Write opening and closing statements
2	Practice direct examination questions for each side Review possible cross-examination questions your witnesses might be asked. Review cross-examination questions for opposition and anticipate what their answers might be Practice delivery of opening and closing statements If possible, visit courtroom to familiarize participants with setting
1 1/2 to 2 hours	Choose and impanel jury Conduct mock trial After trial, discuss results with jury and spectators
1 to 2	With mock trial participants: View tape Evaluate trial specifics

Community Involvement

You will find that it is not difficult to get help with your mock trial from professionals involved in law enforcement. One word of caution—these individuals are very busy. Allow plenty of time for them to arrange their schedules to accommodate you. If you hope to have professionals work with your students, contact them at least 4–6 weeks before you hope to stage your trial. Here are some individuals you might want to contact:

- *Local police chief or sheriff:* Ours proved invaluable. He made arrangements for us to use our town's municipal courtroom for the trial. Each time we planned a trial, he contacted a local or county judge to officiate. If your police chief or sheriff can't help in this area, he may be able to point you in the direction of someone who can.

- *Local attorneys:* Many are more than willing to talk to your students about the legal system and help with formulating direct- and cross-examination questions. If you cannot get a local judge to officiate, you might find a willing attorney to act in this capacity.

- *Bar associations:* Contact your county bar association to see if your state bar association is one of many that hold mock trial competitions on the high school level. They may send you materials on these mock trials and perhaps a videotape of a trial competition that would allow your students to see a mock trial in progress. Be aware that some of the subject matter covered in these trials may not be suitable for younger students. Some bar associations have programs for elementary and middle school students, although they probably will not have actual mock trials for this level.

- *County courthouse:* Check with the nearest county courthouse to see if they allow field trips. These are usually quite popular and may have to be arranged several months in advance. This allows the students to see courtroom procedures in action. Unfortunately, you will not know what the students will see until that day—it all depends what trials or activities are scheduled. We have found that everyone at the courthouse was extremely cooperative and the students gained a great deal from the experience.

CHAPTER 4

Conducting a Mock Trial

Certain procedures and rules are standard when conducting any trial. The following materials are presented in a format that is easy for students to understand. The suggested courtroom layout (Figure 2) is similar to that used in courtrooms throughout the country. It is simple to set up in your classroom or in a roomier environment such as an auditorium if you expect to have a larger audience. Don't overlook the possibility that your local municipal court may be available to you. I was able to arrange the use of our town's court, and it made my class' trials truly memorable experiences.

The following pages present reproducible handouts you can use in your classroom to teach your students about the workings of trials. If possible, duplicate all or part of these materials for your students. This information can serve as your text for teaching about these areas and makes an excellent reference source should questions arise as your mock trial planning gets under way.

The "Anatomy of a Trial" handout (see p. 30) will take you step by step through the various stages of your trial. This includes courtroom procedure and the order in which opening statements, questioning of witnesses, and closing arguments are made.

The "Simplified Rules of Evidence and Procedure" (see p. 32) handout gives detailed information for formulating questions and presenting evidence.

Opening and Closing Statements

Students serving as attorneys will need to prepare opening and closing statements for the mock trial. You may want to pick students with excellent memories

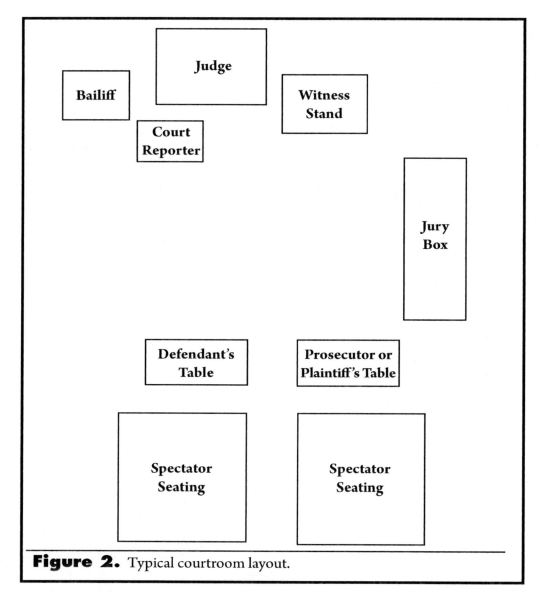

Figure 2. Typical courtroom layout.

and good extemporaneous speaking skills for these roles. More details on opening and closing statements follow, along with a sample affidavit and opening and closing statements for the trial related to that affidavit.

Opening Statements

The purpose of the opening statement is to introduce to the jury the facts of the trial. The prosecution or plaintiff's attorney will present the reasons why a suit has been brought against the plaintiff. When stating the facts, they will use wording that will reflect positively on their viewpoint of the action taken. Conversely, the defendant's lawyer will present the case in support of his client(s). Both attorneys will tell the jury which witnesses they will introduce and what they hope will be the final verdict.

Closing Arguments

When the attorneys present their closing statements, they review the facts that have been presented and reinforce why the facts they have presented support their side. They also, whenever possible, refute the opposition's viewpoint. Finally, they ask that the jury find in their favor. For mock trial purposes, each opening and closing statement should be between 2–5 minutes in length.

Examples of Opening Statements and Closing Arguments

It may be beneficial to students to see what a sample opening and closing statement would look like. Figure 3 presents an affidavit for a hypothetical case. This is similar to the documents students will be analyzing as they present the case. Figures 4 and 5 include examples of opening statements and closing arguments that might have been presented in the hypothetical case of *Penelope Clodhopper v. General Hospital*. For demonstration purposes, we have given the opening statement as it might be presented by the plaintiff's attorney and the closing argument as it might be given by the defendant's lawyer. *Remember that each side delivers an opening statement and a closing argument.*

After reading and reviewing Figures 4 and 5, the differing viewpoints should be readily apparent. The plaintiff's attorney asserts that General Hospital was negligent in providing for the safety of visitors. They should have provided transportation from the parking lot to the front entrance and maintenance should have made sure that there were no icy areas where people walking could fall. They should be held liable for Ms. Clodhopper's injuries. The defense attorney alleges that the plaintiff, Ms. Clodhopper, was irresponsible and did not follow signs directing her to the main entrance of the hospital. By ignoring them and going to the entrance marked "Employees Only," she did not use reasonable caution and was responsible for her own welfare. Each attorney has taken the same facts and stated them in a way that is favorable to his or her client.

IN THE CIRCUIT COURT OF THE THIRD CIRCUIT COURT IN AND FOR JONES COUNTY

PENELOPE CLODHOPPER,
Plaintiff,
-vs-   CASE NO.: 89-375CA
GENERAL HOSPITAL,
 Defendant.

STATEMENT OF FACTS

Around 4 p.m. on January 5, Penelope Clodhopper arrived at General Hospital in Midville to visit her friend, Chauncy Dinwitty. The parking lot was crowded and she had to park a distance from the main entrance of the hospital. It had snowed a few days before and there were piles of plowed snow in the parking lot and along the sidewalks. As she walked toward the front door, she noticed another entrance on the side of the building. It was much closer and if she used it, she would not have to walk in the cold winter air.

The morning had been quite warm and much of the snow had melted. As the sun set, the water from the melting snow had formed a thin film of ice on the pavement. Ms. Clodhopper hurried toward the side door. As she neared it, she saw a sign that read "Employees Only." She stopped but then thought that everyone would understand if she used this entrance so she could get in out of the cold wintry blasts. She rushed ahead and did not see a frozen patch of ice, which was a result of the freezing melted runoff. She slipped and fell, hitting her back and head on the pavement. It was several minutes before someone came out of the building and found her. A stretcher was called for and she was wheeled into the emergency room. As a result of her fall, she broke three ribs and had a mild concussion. Her arm was also injured when she tried to break the fall.

Ms. Clodhopper is charging that management at General Hospital did not take precautions to make sure that visitors to the hospital could safely go from the parking lot to the main building. There were no regular shuttle buses to take passengers from their vehicle to the main entrance of the hospital. Instead, visitors had to walk a great distance. In Ms. Clodhopper's case, she claims she had to walk over 1/4 of a mile. In addition, she claims the hospital's maintenance department had been negligent in assuring that walkways were safe from slippery conditions. Accumulated snow piles had not been removed and salt apparently had not been put on the sidewalks to prevent ice from forming

The management at the General Hospital claims that if Ms. Clodhopper had used the main entrance specified for visitors, the accident would not have happened. The employees' entrance was meant solely for hospital staff members. The sidewalk where Ms. Clodhopper slipped was to the side of the door and not used by hospital personnel who usually walked straight out to their parked vehicles. They maintain that Ms. Clodhopper was responsible for her own safety. By ignoring the entrance that visitors were directed to use, she placed herself at risk.

Figure 3. Affidavit for hypothetical case.

Sample Opening Statement of Plaintiff's Attorney

Ladies and gentlemen of the jury, the plaintiff, Penelope Clodhopper, is here today, not only on her own behalf, but to make sure that others do not suffer injuries because of the inefficiency, thoughtlessness, and carelessness of the management of General Hospital. They would have you believe that Ms. Clodhopper was responsible for her own injuries. Let us look at the facts:

The plaintiff, Penelope Clodhopper, had come to General Hospital to visit her dear friend, Chauncy Dinwitty. She arrived at the hospital parking lot around 4 p.m. Parking spaces close to the hospital were filled, and she had to park a distance of 1/4 mile from the main entrance. She looked around for some ground transportation that might have been provided by the hospital, but there was none. She started to walk towards the main entrance.

It was 4 o'clock in the afternoon on January 5. You know how cold it can get here in Midville on a winter's afternoon. The sun had just about set. As she was walking to the main entrance, Ms. Clodhopper noticed the employees' entrance to General Hospital. It was much closer than the main entrance. Although designated for employees, we will show that hospital visitors regularly use it as a shortcut. This entrance is on the east side of the hospital, so it had been in the shade for several hours. Earlier in the day, the sun had shone there and had caused piles of plowed snow to melt. When this snow melted it left water on the sidewalk near this entrance. As the shade enveloped the area, the water froze, leaving a thin film of ice, which is sometimes referred to as "black ice." Although this ice is merely a film, it can be extremely slippery, as Ms. Clodhopper discovered to her detriment.

We will show that the hospital's maintenance department was negligent in not being more aware of conditions around the hospital, especially with regard to melting snow.

We will show that Ms. Clodhopper was trying to take the shortest path because of poor conditions in the parking lot and the cold temperature.

We will show that the management of General Hospital did not take measures to ensure the safety of visitors. You will see that according to statistics, most hospitals run shuttle buses if the parking lot is large and visitors have to walk a long distance.

We will show that while Ms. Clodhopper was injured as a result of the dangerous conditions due to the hospital's negligence, it could just as easily have been one of the employees who were directed to use the specific entrance in question. Management has exhibited a callous disregard for all individuals, staff and visitors, who enter the hospital through the various entrances provided.

We are sure when you review the facts, you will agree that General Hospital should be held responsible and pay for Ms. Clodhopper's medical costs and pain and suffering.

Figure 4. Opening statement for hypothetical case.

Sample Closing Argument for Defendant's Attorney

Ladies and Gentlemen of the jury, every day we see signs around us that direct us. We go to department stores, supermarkets, airports—the doors are clearly marked "In" and "Out." Why is this done? It is done to make traffic flow more smoothly and to make it safer for the general public. At a hospital, this is doubly important. We not only want to make traffic flow smoothly, but we also want to ensure the security for our patients and staff. By using this main entrance, visitors must go through the main lobby and stop at the reception desk before they can go to elevators and have access to patient areas. The employees' entrance is just that—an entrance for hospital staff and personnel to enter General Hospital.

Ms. Penelope Clodhopper ignored this fact when she opted to try to enter the employees' entrance. Unfortunately, she suffered the consequences of this decision.

You heard Ms Clodhopper state that she had to walk a distance from her parking space to the visitors' entrance and that she did not understand why the hospital had not provided a shuttle bus. We have showed you why management of General Hospital, after careful deliberation, had very good reasons when they decided against making such transportation available

We have proved that security is provided in the parking lot, which is regularly patrolled by trained personnel in marked vehicles.

We have shown official records to prove that temperatures on the day of the incident were not a factor in causing conditions contributing to Ms. Clodhopper's fall.

After reviewing the real facts in this case, we are sure you will understand that Ms. Clodhopper's decision to use the banned entrance was a deciding factor in her accident.

Ladies and gentlemen, we know that you will consider that sometimes there are accidents that are unavoidable, and furthermore, that sometimes an individual's carelessness can be a contributing factor in an accident. Building maintenance departments, whether they are in a commercial building or a hospital, are generally dedicated to making a building as clean and as safe as possible. This is their job.

It is so easy to look for the "deep pockets" to pay for one's own carelessness. This is what drives up insurance rates and, in our case, hospital fees. Look at the facts carefully and we know you will clearly see that General Hospital did nothing wrong and that Ms. Clodhopper, by choosing to use an entrance specifically designated for employees—not for visitors—contributed to her own injuries.

Figure 5. Closing argument for hypothetical case.

Preparing Students to Begin a Mock Trial

After the class reviews the trial procedures and the rules for conducting a trial, students are ready to begin their courtroom experience. To begin work on a particular trial, copies of the "Statement of Facts" and all of the affidavits for that trial should be distributed to students.

Please note that in all of the trials except *United States of America v. Susan B. Anthony,* the state name has been left blank on the official documents. This allows you to add your own choice of state to personalize the trial. In addition, some of the affidavits have provisions for a notary public. You can appoint one of the students who is not an attorney to serve in this capacity.

To begin preparation for the trial, read to the class the background information given for that trial. After this, have the students take turns reading the "Statement of Facts" and the affidavits out loud. After the students have a feel for the individuals and issues involved, ask them to select possible roles they might like to take. Having students list at least two choices makes it easier to make the final selections based on the requests and abilities of the students. Keep in mind that, although it is important to have able attorneys, your witnesses will have to withstand the onslaught of cross-examination and therefore must also be verbally adept.

Once these selections have been made, the two opposing groups will need to prepare for the trial independently in separate locations in the classroom—or, ideally, at separate sites.

Anatomy of a Trial

Court Session Begins

The opening of the court session includes the following events, in the order listed:

1. The bailiff calls the court to order. (Example: "All rise, the court for the City of Riverton is now in session, the Honorable (judge's name) presiding.")
2. The judge enters and all participants remain standing until they are instructed to be seated.
3. The case is announced. (Example: "The court will now hear the case of _____ _____ v. _____.")
4. The judge may tell the jury the specific facts of the case and then ask the attorneys if they are ready to present their cases.

Opening Statements

Opening statements are addressed to the jury. The prosecutor or the plaintiff's attorney summarizes the evidence that will be presented to prove the charge made against the defendant. The defendant's attorney summarizes for the court the evidence that will be presented in answer to the charge the prosecutor or the plaintiff's attorney has made.

Direct Examination by Prosecution or Plaintiff's Attorney

The prosecution or plaintiff's attorney will call to the stand its own witnesses to support its case. At this time, testimony and other evidence will be presented to prove the case. Direct examination allows witnesses to answer questions in narrative form and present facts to support the case.

Cross-Examination by the Defendant's Attorney

The defendant's attorney may cross-examine each witness after the opposing attorney has completed direct examination. The purpose of cross-examination is to clarify or cast doubt upon the testimony of opposing witnesses. Only information presented in sworn affidavits and in direct examination testimony may be used to ask cross-examination questions.

Direct Examination by the Defendant's Attorney

The defendant's attorney will call to the stand its own witnesses to support its case. The defendant may or may not take the stand. Direct examination format is similar to the process used for the prosecution or plaintiff's witnesses.

Cross-Examination by the Prosecution's or Plaintiff's Attorney

Cross-examination of defense witnesses follows the pattern used in cross-examination of prosecution or plaintiff's witnesses.

Closing Arguments

As with opening statements, the closing arguments are addressed to the jury. During the prosecution's closing argument, the evidence presented is reviewed. The attorney points out how the evidence and testimony presented supports the charge against the defendant. Any law applicable in the case is also presented. The attorney for the prosecution asks for a finding of guilty. The plaintiff's attorney asks the jury to find in favor of the plaintiff.

During the defense's closing arguments, the defense also reviews the evidence presented. They indicate how it *does not* support the charge or claim against the defendant. The attorney for the defendant asks for a verdict of not guilty in a criminal case or to find in favor of the defense in a civil trial.

Rendering a Verdict

There are six members on each mock trial jury plus two alternates. If the alternates are not needed, they are dismissed before deliberations begin.

In a criminal trial, the burden of proof rests with the prosecution. They must prove "beyond a reasonable doubt" that the defendant is guilty of the crime. The verdict of the jury must be *unanimous.*

The jury in a civil trial must weigh the evidence. A decision should be reached by a *preponderance of the evidence.* The jury must decide whether the evidence supports the plaintiff's claim or the defendant's claim. A verdict need not be unanimous, but must be agreed to by four or five of the six jurors. (States may have different requirements, check to find what is the practice for your state). Sometimes the jury is asked to place a monetary value on a decision that is rendered in favor of a plaintiff. In some cases, the judge may issue an injunction ordering an individual to refrain from doing a specific act.

Simplified Rules of Evidence and Procedure

Lawyers spend many years training for trials in the courtroom. Procedures can be quite complicated. Listed below are rules for questioning and presenting evidence that have been modified for mock trial participants.

Direct Examination

In direct examination, attorneys question their own witnesses to help support their case.

Form of Questions

Witnesses may not be asked leading questions by the attorney who calls them. A leading question is one in which the attorney supplies information and the answer is usually a "yes" or "no." Direct questions are usually phrased to elicit facts from the witness. They usually begin with the words "who," "what," "where," "when," "why," "how," or "explain."

Example of a direct question: "Mrs. Smith, where did you live before you moved to New Haven?"

Example of a leading question: "Mrs. Smith, isn't it true that you lived at 403 Main Street in Appleton before you moved to New Haven?"

Narration

The purpose of direct examination is to have the witness tell a story; however, care must be taken to ask for specific information.

Example of a narrative question: "Mrs. Smith, why did you move to New Haven?"

Scope of Witness Examination

Direct examination may cover all of the facts relevant to the case of which the witness has firsthand knowledge. For mock trial purposes, information contained in the witness affidavits may be used as a basis for determining this.

Cross-Examination

In the cross-examination stage, attorneys question the witnesses called by their opposing attorneys. This helps negate any evidence brought by the opposing side.

Form of Questions

An attorney may ask leading questions when cross-examining the opponent's witnesses. Narrative questions should be avoided. The ideal answer to a leading question is 'yes" or "no." Should the witness not answer what is anticipated, the attorney should be prepared to ask a question to disprove the response. Attorneys should be careful not to ask a question on cross-examination if they do not know what the witness's answer will be.

Example of a leading question: "Mr. Tompkins, you had a lot to gain if Mr. Sherman lost his job, didn't you?" "No" is the anticipated answer. Should the witness answer, "Yes," the attorney could ask, "Mr. Tompkins, isn't it true that you were next in line to become District Manager?" (This question should be asked only if there is information in affidavits or exhibits to prove Tompkins would benefit.)

Scope of Witness Examination

Attorneys may only ask questions about information brought out in direct examination or to matters relating to the credibility of the witness. For mock trial purposes, questions may be asked on cross-examination about any information that is in a witness's affidavit.

Impeachment

The attorney conducting the cross examination may want to show that the witness should not be believed. This may be done by asking questions that make the witness's truth-telling ability doubtful.

Refreshing Recollection

Impeachment also may be done by introducing the witness's affidavit and having the witness read the portion of the affidavit that was contradicted on direct or cross-examination. The witness may then be questioned about any discrepancies. (For example, if Tompkins said, "No" to the above question, his affidavit stating that he was next in line for promotion after Sherman could be introduced.)

Additional Rules of Evidence

Hearsay

A statement made by someone who is not present in court that is offered to prove the truth of a fact, a piece of evidence, or any witness's testimony is hearsay and not permitted.

Example: A witness states: "The people in my office have told me that Mrs. Lee was fired from her past job because she was always absent."

Opinions of Witnesses

Usually, witnesses are not allowed to state their opinions. An exception to this rule would be a witness who is qualified as an "expert." The attorney who calls this witness is the one who must bring out on direct examination the background that would qualify the witness as an expert.

Relevance of Evidence

Only testimony and physical evidence that is important to the case may be presented. For example, asking a witness's age on cross examination would be allowed only if his or her age is relevant to the case.

Introduction of Physical Evidence

Only objects and documents that are relevant to the case may be introduced. Before the trial, each side must permit the opposing side to examine any piece of evidence (exhibit) that will be introduced. During the actual trial, each piece of evidence is introduced immediately prior to its use in questioning. The evidence is presented to the judge. "Your Honor, I offer this letter for admission as evidence." At this point, the judge will examine the evidence, label it (P1 for the prosecution or plaintiff or D1 for the defense, with the numbers increasing with each additional piece of evidence). The exhibit is then returned to the attorney who will show it to the opposing counsel. At this point, questioning may continue. Affidavits are not admissible as evidence but may be used during cross-examination for impeachment purposes.

Objections

Only student attorneys may object at any time they believe the opposition has violated the rules of evidence. *Objections are made directly to the judge and must be made immediately at the time the attorney believes the violation has occurred.* Some of the standard objections that may be made include:

- *Irrelevant evidence:* "I object, your Honor. This testimony is irrelevant to the facts of the case."
- *Leading question:* "Objection. Counsel is leading the witness." This may only be used if an attorney is using leading questions on direct examination.
- *Hearsay:* "Objection. The question or answer is based on hearsay."
- *Opinion:* "Objection. Counsel is asking the witness to give an opinion."

Mock trials move very rapidly. Student lawyers have little experience in being able to recognize testimony that might be subject to an objection. To help them become more proficient, the teacher working with them might consider doing practice testimony that would elicit objections.

Part III: The Trials

CHAPTER 5

Criminal Trials

Criminal courts deal with individuals accused of crimes. All crimes are considered as offenses against the government in that they violate laws meant to ensure domestic tranquility. A district attorney or state attorney usually handles the prosecution in such trials. Although the courts are considered a branch of the government, they are neutral in trials between the prosecution and the defense.

In the United States, a defendant is presumed innocent until proven guilty. It is the prosecution that bears the burden of proof. The defendant usually employs an attorney to represent his interest. Should the defendant be unable to afford such counsel, a court appointed public defender will ensure that the accused receives legal representation.

Trials held in criminal courts are usually held before a jury who determines whether the accused is guilty or not guilty. The jury may consist of either 6 or 12 jurors with several alternates sworn in should a jury member be unable to hear the entire trial. The decision in a criminal trial must be unanimous. (The jury ballot reads "SO SAY WE ALL:" after which the jury foreman signs and dates the ballot to represent the entire jury's decision.) The jury must return a not guilty verdict if there is a reasonable doubt of the defendant's guilt. Acquittal is justified if there is doubt based on reason and arising from evidence or lack of evidence.

The jury also may be called upon to decide what the punishment will be, although it is more often determined by the judge presiding over the trial.

The following trials deal with individuals who have been accused of breaking the law. They have been charged with an assorted crimes—influencing the outcome of a sporting event, illegal betting, and registering and voting illegally.

- *The State v. Gerry Rabbitt and Lu Fox* is based on the fable "The Tortoise and the Hare." This trial is placed in a modern setting. Rabbitt and Fox are accused of fixing the results of a race and having placed bets on the outcome. Teachers, the names of the minor characters are ambiguous, allowing either male or female students to play the characters. You may change the pronouns on the affidavits if you choose to have a student of the gender opposite to what is mentioned play the role.
- *The United States v. Susan B. Anthony* is based on an actual trial. In 1872, Susan B. Anthony and several other women were arrested for voting illegally. Women had not been given the right to vote and wouldn't be granted that privilege until 1920. The trial was held, but the judge rendered a verdict of guilty without letting the defendants testify and without allowing the jury to deliberate. An appeal was denied. *In our trial, we are rewriting history and allowing the verdict to be appealed.*

The State v. Gerry Rabbitt and Lu Fox

Background Information

  This trial places the fabled race of the Tortoise and the Hare in a modern-day setting. The town of Forest Lakes was having a 3-day Bicentennial celebration over the Labor Day weekend. As a highlight of the event, a race was arranged between two of the town's favorite athletes, Jamie Tortoise and Gerry Rabbitt. The winner of the race would receive a large trophy and bragging rights.

  Jamie Tortoise is a retired minor league baseball player. When he played, he was a slow runner, but very crafty. His expertise helped him set a league record for stolen bases because opposing teams underestimated his base running ability. His nickname was "Slow and Steady."

  Gerry Rabbitt is an Olympic racer and has set records in both sprints and longer races. He is highly regarded as a runner who trains hard and does his best in every race.

  Town officials had applied to the state for permission to set up legalized betting solely for this event. The request was denied. Some townspeople were disappointed, but others felt this was a family event and gambling should not be allowed.

  The course for the race was 3 miles long. Its path led the two runners through the woods and around the lakes surrounding Forest Lakes. The town was too small to have it any other way. When the route was laid out, it was determined that the runners could be monitored for most of the race. The first two miles were viewed by a judge's car that followed the runners. Then, the trail became too narrow for the car to continue. This section of the race was dubbed the

"Bermuda Triangle" because of its inaccessibility and to give it an air of mystery. The spotter for this section was Lu Fox.

Gerry Rabbitt claims that at this point of the race he met Lu Fox. They chatted briefly and then Lu left. Rabbitt claims he decided to slow down and rest so that he would not win by too large a margin. Unfortunately, when he sat down, he nodded off. When he awoke, he realized that some time had gone by and he was not sure where Jamie Tortoise was. He started running only to see Tortoise nearing the finish line. Rabbitt ran as fast as possible but could not beat Tortoise.

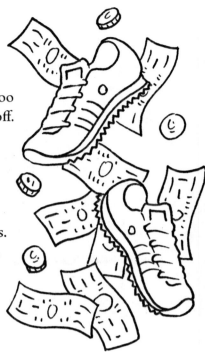

Tortoise states that he saw Rabbitt and Fox talking as he passed. They were deep in conversation and did not see him pass. Tortoise felt his winning was another example of the opposition underestimating him.

Later it was discovered that Lu Fox allegedly bet a large amount of money on Tortoise to win the race and that Lu Fox deposited $19,500 to his personal checking account after the race.

Police Chief Sam Hawkins questioned Fox and Rabbitt, and after reviewing the evidence and statements of other witnesses, Hawkins charged them both with illegal gambling and charged Rabbitt with illegally affecting the outcome of a sporting event.

The names of the witnesses in this trial may be either male or female. It is probably preferred to have Gerry Rabbitt and Jamie Tortoise as male because of the fact that there are more male professional athletes; however, if you wish you may identify them as female.

Applicable Law

Influencing the Outcome of a Sporting Event

Whoever knowingly gives, promises, or offers to any professional or amateur athlete or official who participates in any professional or amateur game, contest, or sport any benefit with intent to influence the person to lose or try to lose or to limit the person's or person's team's margin of victory or defeat is guilty of a felony. Any athlete who participates in such an action that would affect the outcome of a sporting event shall also be deemed guilty of the same offense.

Definitions

Bicentennial—a 200th anniversary celebration.
Felony—a serious crime, such as murder, larceny, or robbery, punishable by imprisonment in a state or federal penitentiary. Those convicted of murder may be sentenced to the death penalty in some states.
Making book—taking bets on a contest or sporting event.
Match race—a contest between two individuals.

Exhibits/Materials

- Map of race showing "Bermuda Triangle" section and location of Gerry Rabbitt's alleged nap (optional)
- Poster advertising race (optional)
- Bank statement showing deposit for $19,500 (see Figure 6)

Note: Optional exhibits may be prepared by the students serving as research assistants.

Trial Participants

Prosecution: Attorneys, Jamie Tortoise, Sam Hawkins, Sal Barney
Defense: Attorneys, Gerry Rabbitt (Defendant), Lu Fox (Defendant), Cary O'Hare, Drew Walters

Formulating Questions for Direct and Cross-Examination

The mock trials in this book have been designed to allow for no clear-cut solutions. It is up to the attorneys to explore the affidavits of the opposition for weaknesses and inconsistencies. It is very important that all affidavits be looked at in this way, so that students can prepare for cross-examination. Students should be especially careful to analyze the affidavit of each witness to determine what information is factual and which is opinion. *Opinions are only admissible as testimony if offered by an expert witness.* An example would be a DNA expert who could give an opinion as to whether physical evidence at a crime scene matched the DNA pattern of a person accused of the crime.

I have found it best to allow the students to explore their own ideas first. Then, ask them specific questions and have them suggest possible ways that both the prosecution and defense might approach each question. By doing this the students come to understand that they must look at all aspects of the case from both sides. The sample question below gives possible approaches by the prosecution and the defense.

> *Example:* If Lu Fox actually bet on the race, how could he justify betting such large sums of money unless he knew the outcome of the race was a sure thing?
> *Prosecution:* He couldn't justify it! He saw an opportunity to make a lot of money and also to bring a lot of customers into his sports bar who would want to bet on the race.
> *Defense:* He regarded it as friendly betting and no different from the usual side bets on other sporting events. To him it was an investment to attract new customers who weren't regulars at his sports bar.

You may want to use some of the following questions as guidelines in helping students prepare direct and cross-examination. (Remind the students that an attorney never asks a question on cross-examination unless he or she knows the answer the witness will give.)

- Why did the town officials even consider setting up betting in race in which the competitors were so unevenly matched?
- Could Jamie Tortoise perhaps have been "in" on any alleged plans to throw the race?
- Wasn't a spotter's role in a race to make sure that nothing unusual happened to the runners and that they were on track?
- How could the police be unaware that illegal betting was going on?

- If this was a family event, why would the race planners even consider betting?
- What were Gerry Rabbitt and Lu Fox talking about when they met in the Bermuda Triangle?
- Is it possible that Lu Fox convinced Gerry Rabbitt to "wait a bit" so that the race would be closer and more interesting?
- How would it benefit Gerry Rabbitt to throw the race?
- Lu Fox used a personal checking account to make the deposit. Why not use a business checking account? Does one exist?

Trial Documents

The pages that follow include a statement of facts about the trial, affidavits from each witness, and forms for the jury to determine guilt or innocence. These forms are reproducible and should be given to all students helping to prepare for the trial. You may also wish to make copies of the bank statement (Figure 6) available to them.

Forest Lakes National Bank
346 Pine Trail
Forest Lakes

Lu Fox
1219 Maple Avenue
Forest Lakes

ACCOUNT # 4486271234

Personal Checking Account
August 15 through September 14

SUMMARY	
Beginning Balance	$ 2,674.89
Deposits & Credits	$23,432.64 +
Withdrawals	$ 150.00 -
Fees	$ 10.00 -
Checks	$ 4,071.14 -
Ending Balance	$21,876.39

DEPOSITS & CREDITS

Date		
8/15	Deposit—Thank you	375.55
8/18	Deposit—Thank you	692.20
8/22	Deposit—Thank you	766.86
8/26	Deposit—Thank you	513.03
8/30	Deposit—Thank you	520.00
9/02	Deposit—Thank you	442.00
9/03	Deposit—Thank you	623.00
9/06	Deposit—Thank you	19,500.00
	Total Deposits & Credits	**$23,432.64**

WITHDRAWALS & FEES

Date		
8/24	ATM Withdrawal Forest Lakes National Bank	150.00
8/30	Monthly Service Charge	10.00
	Total Withdrawals & Fees	**$160.00**

CHECKS

Date	Check No.	Amount
8/16	489	1,301.14
8/18	490	820.00
8/20	491	950.00
9/01	492	1,000.00
	Total Checks	**$4,071.14**

Figure 6. Bank statement for Lu Fox.

IN THE CIRCUIT COURT OF THE EIGHTH JUDICIAL CIRCUIT,
IN AND FOR JOHNSON COUNTY, _____

THE STATE OF _____
 Plaintiff
-v-   CASE NO.: 12-345-CF
GERRY RABBITT and
LU FOX
Defendants

STATEMENT OF FACTS

The town of Forest Lakes had planned a huge celebration for the town's bicentennial celebration. Proceeds of the event would go to building a new library.

There were to be the usual contests and rides that would create a fair-like atmosphere. The highlight of the 3-day celebration was to be a match race between two of the town's most celebrated athletes—Olympic racer Gerry Rabbit and former baseball player, Jamie Tortoise. Planners wanted to use this event as a means for attracting people to the fair. Rabbitt had won and set records in many Olympic events—both short sprints and longer endurance races. Tortoise was noted for base running expertise, not necessarily as the fastest runner, but as a crafty runner able to fool the opposing team. This resulted in Tortoise leading the league in stolen bases.

Town officials applied to the state for permission to set up legalized betting on the race but the state refused to allow them to do so.

The race was set for a distance of 3 miles, meandering through the woods and around the lakes for which the town was named. There would be spotters along the way. Because some of the route was on narrow lanes not accessible by car, these spotters would have to serve as monitors for the more inaccessible areas. The winner of the race would receive a trophy and bragging rights.

At the beginning of the race, everyone thought that the Olympic racer Rabbitt would win the race. The two competitors lined up and were off and running at the sound of the starter's pistol. The younger Rabbitt raced out ahead as the veteran Tortoise followed, keeping a slow and steady pace. A judge's car followed the two runners for about the first 2 miles. At this point, Jamie Tortoise could not see Rabbitt, who was far ahead. Not one to give up easily, his steady plodding pace was continued. After 2 miles, the road narrowed and the car could no longer follow.

At this point, the two runners gave different versions of what had happened. Rabbitt claimed that being so far ahead, and not wanting to deliver a crushing blow to the opposing runner, he stopped to talk briefly to spotter Lu

Fox. After Lu Fox left, Rabbitt still had not seen Jamie Tortoise so he sat off to the side of the road to give the competition a chance to catch up. Because Rabbitt was sitting on the opposite side of a tree, he claims that Jamie Tortoise could not have seen him. Rabbitt says he fell asleep because of the long wait for Tortoise to go by. Rabbitt awoke with a start and ran valiantly, but was about 2 feet behind as Jamie Tortoise crossed the finish line. Gerry Rabbitt had lost.

Tortoise claimed to have seen Rabbitt when he ran by but did not acknowledge him. Tortoise claims that Rabbitt was standing by a tree talking to one of the spotters, Lu Fox.

Sal Barney testified to seeing Lu Fox "flashing a lot of money after the race." Drew Walters said that it was common knowledge that someone was making book on the race and many people had placed bets.

The officials discussed the situation with the two runners and began an investigation. Gerry Rabbitt was charged with collaborating with Lu Fox to throw the race. It was alleged that Fox had bet heavily on Tortoise to win the race and had shared the winnings with Rabbitt. Cary O'Hare, who had been Rabbitt's high school track coach and trainer for the Olympics, said that Rabbitt had been an excellent student and competitor and would never jeopardize a sports career by participating in a betting scandal.

The defendants, Gerry Rabbitt and Lu Fox, have been charged with influencing the outcome of a sporting event. Lu Fox has been charged with illegal betting.

IN THE CIRCUIT COURT OF THE EIGHTH JUDICIAL CIRCUIT, IN AND FOR JOHNSON COUNTY, _____

THE STATE OF _____
 Plaintiff

-v-   CASE NO.: 12-345-CF

GERRY RABBITT and
LU FOX
Defendants

GENERAL AFFIDAVIT

<u>Jamie Tortoise</u>, being first duly sworn according to law, deposes and says that:

I had a long career in baseball and although I never played in the majors, I was a legend in my own way. I learned very young when I was in grammar school that I would never win a race by speed, so I had to figure out other ways. I remember my physical education teacher telling me that I should give up any ideas of winning track meets or being a baseball player. My dad told me that I should always do my very best no matter what I was doing. So, I would run as fast as I could and never stop along the way.

When I first started baseball, the pitcher and catcher paid no attention to me because they knew I was such a slow runner. I was called "slow and steady." When I stole my first base, everyone was surprised. They thought it was just luck because they hadn't been paying attention. Then, I stole a second and a third. My reputation spread throughout the league until pitchers and catchers became nervous when I got on base. They made errors and I quickly became the talk of the league. Only the very best players were able to get me out. You might say I "psyched out" the others.

When the town leaders of Forest Lakes approached me about the race against Gerry Rabbitt, I at first declined. Then, Rabbitt started ribbing me and I decided to show that I could win no matter how many records for speed he had set.

I was glad when the state turned down the proposal to have betting on the race. This was to be a family event and having organized gambling was not a good example for the town's children.

The day of the race was beautiful, and when we began Rabbitt took a big lead right away. I kept my usual pace: slow and steady. One of the pace cars followed me until we got to the narrow path where it could no longer follow. I continued on. I heard voices and when I looked around I saw Gerry and Lu talking by a tree. I thought nothing of it. I knew Lu was there as a spotter. I also was used to people thinking I would never win, so they took chances. In this case, Gerry claims he didn't want to beat me by too much. Could be. Many have slacked off and underestimated me.

Gerry says that I was not seen by either of them. There were some fairly high bushes near the tree and I will admit that I ran as quietly as I could and ducked down until I was out of their sight. Even so, they were so intense in their conversation, I doubt they would have seen me if I had run in my usual manner. I continued running and fully expected that Gerry would pass me at any time. I saw the finish line and ran as fast as I could. The crowd was cheering so loudly that I didn't even hear Gerry crossing the line just a few steps behind me.

Gerry didn't appear to be too upset, but I figured it was just good sportsmanship. I was awarded a big trophy for my win. A while later, I saw the race officials in a huddle. Then, I heard there was some illegal betting. I figured it was something like the "office pool" where people bet on the Super Bowl or World Series. Technically, it's illegal, but everyone does it. Then, the police chief showed up and a lot of people were questioned. Turns out the betting was widespread and large amounts of money were involved. Naturally, Gerry was a big favorite and no one expected me to win. The odds were something like 30 to 1 for me to win and 2 to 1 for Gerry to win. For every dollar you bet on me, you won $30. If you bet $10, you won $300; if you bet $100, you won $3,000.

Then, it was reported that Lu Fox had bet a large amount of money and was bragging about it. When they questioned me, I mentioned that I had seen Lu and Gerry talking as I passed by. After that, the police questioned Gerry and Lu and arrested them. Lu Fox was charged with illegal gambling, and Gerry and Lu were both charged with illegally affecting the outcome of the race. I find this hard to believe. Gerry has a reputation of working hard. I don't believe that jeopardizing a future in competitive running would be worth throwing a race. But, you never know. Sometimes the temptation of a sure thing can tempt even the most upstanding individual.

_____

Affiant

SWORN TO AND SUBSCRIBED before me this _____ day of
_____ in this year_____

_____

NOTARY PUBLIC

State of _____

My Commission Expires: _____

IN THE CIRCUIT COURT OF THE EIGHTH JUDICIAL CIRCUIT, IN AND FOR JOHNSON COUNTY, _____

THE STATE OF _____
 Plaintiff
-v-
GERRY RABBITT and
LU FOX
Defendants

CASE NO.: 12-345-CF

GENERAL AFFIDAVIT

<u>Sam Hawkins, Chief of Police, Forest Lakes</u>, being first duly sworn according to law, deposes and says that:

I am a native of Forest Lakes. I went to school here and only left for 4 years to go to the state university. After graduation, I returned here and decided to make a career in law enforcement. At first, I started as a police officer. We had a three-man force then, including the chief. After about 8 years, the police chief retired and I applied for his job. Because I was the only candidate with a degree in criminal justice, I got the position. Since I took over as chief 4 years ago, the force has increased to six officers and myself. We feel we have an extraordinary group of individuals helping to make the citizens of Forest Lakes safe and secure.

When the committee started to plan this event, I sat in on some of the meetings. When the idea of betting on the match race between Gerry Rabbitt and Jamie Tortoise was brought up, I cautioned that they had better check into state regulations about betting. We wanted to make everything legal. Turns out, it was a good thing we did investigate this further, because the state said we had to make a formal application. We did and quickly got a reply denying our request for legal betting. This was widely known and a lot of people were upset because they thought betting would make the event more interesting.

The route for the race was drawn up. When I saw it, I suggested that the area to be known as the "Bermuda Triangle" could be a problem. Everyone laughed and said it added an air of mystery. After all, the race was really just a fun event.

I drove the pace car at the beginning of the race and I stayed behind Jamie Tortoise. Gerry Rabbitt was way ahead. I drove as far as the narrow part of the route until I could no longer see Jamie. I then detoured back to the main road and arrived at the finish line. I fully expected to see Rabbitt standing there, but he was nowhere to be seen. I looked around, thinking that maybe Rabbitt had finished so far ahead and had gone off to get a cool drink. Then, I saw Tortoise come out of the thicket, moving as fast as possible, which wasn't very fast. Approaching the finish line, Tortoise had a determined look. Suddenly, there was a flurry of activity and Gerry Rabbitt came into view, crossing the finish line a few feet behind Jamie.

At first, Gerry appeared upset, but then, showing good sportsmanship, he handed the winning trophy to Jamie.

I went back to my command post to see how security was progressing. One of the officers said that he had heard people were upset and it was rumored that there had been illegal betting. I commented that perhaps it was just a few people making side bets, but then he said he had heard it was widespread.

Shortly after that, Sal Barney called me on my cell phone, wanting to discuss something important immediately. I drove over to where Barney was and heard that Lu Fox had been seen with a large amount of money. Lu had admitted to betting $100 on the race, "just to make things interesting."

When running in the "Bermuda Triangle" portion of the race, Jamie Tortoise said that Fox and Rabbitt were standing next to a tree, talking. Tortoise said it was doubtful that they saw the opposition running by, they were so deep in conversation. Rabbitt and Fox acknowledge the conversation, but deny there was a conspiracy to allow Tortoise to win so they could split what Fox had won by betting against Rabbitt.

When we checked the local banks, we found that on the day after the race a deposit in the amount of $19,500 had been made to a personal checking account registered to Lu Fox. It was reported that Lu Fox had made 7 bets of $100 each. With the odds at 30 to 1, the winnings would have totaled $21,000. Because the betting was illegal, no individuals would come forth to admit that they had bet on Gerry Rabbitt to win the race. When questioned about the deposit, Fox said the money came from sports memorabilia that had been sold over the weekend. Fox could not account for the items sold and could not verify who had made the purchases.

I checked the state statutes and found that because the town had been denied a gambling permit, the betting was illegal. Furthermore, doing something to affect the outcome of the race was also against the law.

I then read both Lu Fox and Gerry Rabbitt their rights. Believe me, it was one of the hardest things I've had to do since being in law enforcement.

_____

Affiant

SWORN TO AND SUBSCRIBED before me this _____ day of

_____ in this year _____

_____

NOTARY PUBLIC

State of _____

My Commission Expires: _____

IN THE CIRCUIT COURT OF THE EIGHTH JUDICIAL CIRCUIT,
IN AND FOR JOHNSON COUNTY, _____

THE STATE OF _____
 Plaintiff
-v-   CASE NO.: 12-345-CF
GERRY RABBITT and
LU FOX
Defendants

GENERAL AFFIDAVIT

<u>Sal Barney</u>, being first duly sworn according to law, deposes and says that:

I was named chairman of the Forest Lakes Bicentennial Committee. The committee has been working on this event for more than a year. We wanted to do more than just have a celebration, we wanted it to be something that townspeople would remember for years to come I suggested that perhaps we could use it as a fundraiser. The members of the committee seemed to like the idea and after much discussion, we decided to use the proceeds toward building a new library. Ours is too small for our growing town, and it does not have up-to-date technology. We still have the old card catalog rather than a computerized version.

We needed something to bring in crowds and call attention to the event. Someone suggested we might be able to invite some celebrities. Jamie Tortoise and Gerry Rabbitt immediately came to mind. Both were born and raised here. They no longer live here, but we still regard them as our own. Why, we even have a sign as you enter Forest Lakes that says "Home of Champions—Jamie Tortoise and Gerry Rabbitt."

We thought we would just have them come and make a public appearance, you know, sign autographs and pose for pictures (for a fee, of course). We felt this was a good attraction and would really increase attendance at the celebration. Many of the younger children didn't know them, and this was a chance for them to be introduced to the town's heroes.

Lu Fox, who was a member of the committee, suggested that perhaps we could have a match race between the two athletes. Everyone laughed, because Rabbitt was noted for his speed and Tortoise was slow and plodding. Lu suggested that we contact both of them and see what they had to say. After all, they would know if it would work. Surprisingly, they both agreed.

Lu said that Gerry Rabbitt had suggested that there be betting on the race, similar to that done in horse races. We discussed the idea and Sam Hawkins said we would have to make sure we were not breaking any laws. Sam investigated and found that if we wanted to have betting, we would have to get state approval. We applied to the state and were denied approval. After that, we decided to go back to our original public appearance plan. Gerry called and suggested that the race be held anyway. Even though there would not be any betting, it would still be a good promotion and bring in more people. Tortoise agreed and laughingly suggested we could award a trophy to the winner—one that could be added to the many that were already in Tortoise's collection.

We started promoting the event, hung banners all over town, and advertised it on the local radio and TV stations. We called it the "Race of Champions."

Our celebration lasted 3 days. On the first day, Rabbitt and Tortoise posed for pictures and signed autographs. The proceeds from these appearances were excellent—beyond what we had hoped.

The second day was the race. To make it as authentic as possible, we posted a map of the race course. People volunteered to be "official spotters." We had someone in a car at the beginning of the race. Lu Fox offered to be a spotter in what we called the "Bermuda Triangle" of the race. The kids loved that. It gave the race an added air of mystery. This part of the race was on a secluded trail that was too narrow for a car. It wasn't too far from the end so people could view the runners as they left the "Bermuda Triangle." As soon as the leader came out, a pace car would start up and lead him to the finish line. Everyone was astonished when Jamie appeared first. The crowd went wild. Just as Tortoise approached the finish line, Gerry Rabbitt came roaring into view. It was too late. Rabbitt crossed the line a few steps behind Tortoise. At first, Gerry appeared upset, but then started to laugh good-naturedly and even handed the trophy to Jamie.

Then, the buzz started in the crowd. Everyone found it hard to believe that Tortoise had won. When it came to speed, the two runners weren't even close. Rumors started that Gerry had thrown the race. This was unbelievable. Still, I thought, "It's only a token race. It really doesn't matter." It really was an exciting race, much more so than if Rabbitt had come running in way ahead of Tortoise.

I don't know where Lu Fox was when the race ended, but afterward, Lu showed me a large amount of money, saying, "You know, I bet $100 just to show my customers I was a good sport and to make things interesting. Look what I won!" Many people didn't seem to be too happy with Lu.

I called the police chief and asked if there could be a problem. An investigation was begun. Rabbitt, Tortoise, and Fox were brought in for questioning. As a result, charges were brought against Rabbitt and Fox.

We had wanted this celebration to be something memorable. Turns out people will remember it for all the wrong reasons.

_____
Affiant

SWORN TO AND SUBSCRIBED before me this _____ day of _____ in this year _____

_____
NOTARY PUBLIC
State of _____
My Commission Expires: _____

IN THE CIRCUIT COURT OF THE EIGHTH JUDICIAL CIRCUIT, IN AND FOR JOHNSON COUNTY, _____

THE STATE OF _____
 Plaintiff
-v-   CASE NO.: 12-345-CF
GERRY RABBITT and
LU FOX
Defendants

GENERAL AFFIDAVIT

<u>Gerry Rabbitt</u>, being first duly sworn according to law, deposes and says that:

I have lived in Forest Lakes all of my life. Ever since grammar school, I have loved running. When I got to high school, the track coach introduced me to Cary O'Hare, who had experience as a coach for professional runners. Cary took me aside and told me I was a "natural" and that we should see how far I could go with competitive running. At first I competed in school, then with other schools in the county and then the state tournaments. By this time, I had done so well, we decided to train for the Olympics. Running was everything to me.

When the bicentennial committee asked me to run against Jamie Tortoise, I thought at first that this would be no contest. Sure, Jamie was a good runner and won by outsmarting the competition, but when it came to speed, he poked along compared to me. Then someone explained that this race was to help attract people to the Bicentennial Fair and that it was for a good cause. The town was badly in need of a new library.

At first, they wanted to make a race people could bet on, but the state refused them the license to do so. It was just as well, because this was a race that was for fun and betting would be out of line.

The day of the race, Jamie and I talked before the race. We were kidding each other. Jamie said I was the Whiz Kid and I called him Slow Poke. The Bicentennial Committee spent a lot of time planning the race. The track was not the usual oval because they didn't have one near the fairground. They decided to create a race route that went through the woods to emphasize that this was a town of forests and lakes. I thought that was an interesting idea. At the beginning of the race, we were trailed by officials in a car. When the route got too narrow, they had "official spotters" along the way.

The race began and I shot out ahead. Jamie moved at a fairly good pace, but the thing that I noticed was that the pace was even—no letting up, no bursts of speed—just an even pace.

When I got to the part of the forest that had been named the "Bermuda Triangle," I looked back and Jamie was nowhere to be seen. I really didn't want to win by a huge margin, so I stopped to talk to Lu Fox. I commented that I was amazed that we had such a huge turnout for the race because there was no betting. Lu laughed and said, "Well, not legally. Someone was making book." You know, taking illegal bets. Lu left saying it was too hot and that I should take it easy. That was the last I saw Lu until after the race.

Jamie was still nowhere to be seen. It was hot so I sat down and I guess I dozed off for a few minutes. When I woke up, I realized quite a bit of time had gone by. I started running and could see the finish line and up ahead, there was Jamie! I ran as hard as I could, but Jamie crossed the line before me.

Everyone thought it was a big joke that pokey Jamie Tortoise could beat an Olympic runner. Someone suggested that maybe I threw the race—you know, that I let Jamie win. I just laughed. The race wasn't official, and it was all in good fun.

Then rumors started that there had been a lot of betting on the race— illegal, of course. I still didn't think anything of it. After all, people have "office pools" on the World Series and the Super Bowl and it's all for fun. Then, Lu Fox was bragging about betting on Jamie Tortoise because Jamie had a reputation for outsmarting the opposition. Jamie didn't beat me. I beat myself. I didn't continue doing my best. I didn't run my best race. Jamie would never have won if I had.

Apparently I did not see Jamie go by when I was talking to Lu. That's how he got so far ahead. As for me betting, why would I jeopardize my sports career for a few dollars gained on an illegal bet?

_____

Affiant

SWORN TO AND SUBSCRIBED before me this _____ day of _____ in this year_____

_____

NOTARY PUBLIC

State of _____

My Commission Expires: _____

IN THE CIRCUIT COURT OF THE EIGHTH JUDICIAL CIRCUIT, IN AND FOR JOHNSON COUNTY, _____

THE STATE OF _____
 Plaintiff
-v-
GERRY RABBITT and
LU FOX
Defendants

CASE NO.: 12-345-CF

GENERAL AFFIDAVIT

<u>Lu Fox</u>, being first duly sworn according to law, deposes and says that:

I've lived in Forest Lakes all my life and have been good friends with both Gerry Rabbitt and Jamie Tortoise. When I heard that they were going to have a race, I thought this would be fun and it would bring a lot of people to the town's bicentennial celebration. After all, both of them were famous for being outstanding athletes.

I run a local restaurant and many of the town's people visit on a regular basis. We have a bar, but it is separated from the dining room so that families are not discouraged from dining here. I act as manager, and I often tend to the bar. Whenever there is a major sporting event, this is the place most of the town's people congregate to watch it on TV. There is usually some betting going on, but it is not organized—just between a few friends.

The day of the race, I volunteered to be a spotter. No one really wanted to do the stretch of the race inaccessible by cars, so I offered my services. I saw Gerry come tearing through with Jamie nowhere in sight. Gerry saw me and looked back. Not seeing Jamie, Gerry stopped and we chatted momentarily. We laughed that it was not much of a race and I suggested that perhaps Gerry should wait a bit and let Jamie go by. When Jamie came into sight, Gerry could start running slowly. Then, there could be a photo finish. I left and slowly walked up to near the finish line. I never saw Jamie until I got to the finish line. Jamie was plodding along slow and steady. The crowd was cheering and suddenly Gerry came roaring into view. It was indeed almost a photo finish, and Jamie won the race.

I must say Gerry was a really good sport about it, laughing and patting Jamie on the back. The night before, a group of customers were in my bar and someone suggested that we could have our usual betting pool. I thought it sounded like fun. I knew the state had denied the committee legalized betting, but this was just a little betting between friends. Everyone was betting on Gerry, so to make it interesting, I said I would bet on Jamie. I bet $100. Word spread about the betting and word got out that I had bet on Jamie. Before I knew it someone was making book and everyone was betting. Very few people bet on Jamie. How could he possibly win against an Olympic runner?

The person handling the bets had given odds of 30 to 1 for Jamie—a real long shot. When Jamie won the race, I won $3,000. Boy, was I surprised! Then the word got out to town officials and the police started investigating. They checked my personal checking account and discovered I had deposited $19,500 right after the race. They wanted to know where the money came from. I told them that I had a lot of sports memorabilia at my restaurant—you know signed photos, baseballs, sports jerseys, etc. I'd had these items for a long time. We had a lot of people in the restaurant because of the bicentennial and they seemed interested in them. I thought this might be a good time to sell them. I had planned to redecorate soon any way. The police talked to both Jamie and Gerry and some of my customers and before long, Gerry and I were arrested for illegal betting and for conspiring to influence the outcome of an athletic event.

The fact that Gerry would even consider not doing his best is unbelievable. Gerry may not have wanted to make Jamie look really bad, but it was only a race for fun, not an official event.

As for my betting $100, I just wanted to show everyone I was a good sport and would participate in an event with my customers. That's just good business!

_____
Affiant

SWORN TO AND SUBSCRIBED before me this _____ day of _____ in this year_____

_____
NOTARY PUBLIC
State of _____
My Commission Expires: _____

IN THE CIRCUIT COURT OF THE EIGHTH JUDICIAL CIRCUIT, IN AND FOR JOHNSON COUNTY, _____

THE STATE OF _____
Plaintiff
-v-
GERRY RABBITT and
LU FOX
Defendants

CASE NO.: 12-345-CF

GENERAL AFFIDAVIT

<u>Cary O'Hare</u>, being first duly sworn according to law, deposes and says that:

I first met Gerry Rabbitt at a local track meet. I'd never seen a runner with so much natural talent and energy. From the very first race, Gerry was enthusiastic and really wanted to win. Coming in second was not an option. The only problem was that energy and enthusiasm had to be channeled so the outcome would be a consistent positive performance. We worked on pacing and getting to know the opposing runners. That was an important part of the training. Gerry studied the performance of each competitor and found the weaknesses and strengths that each had.

Gerry participated on a local, county, and state level. The ultimate goal was to prepare for Olympic competition. Gerry knew that doing well in the Olympics could be a springboard to a career in sports as a coach, commentator, or a TV personality. Actually, Gerry was not trained to do anything else. Although he was a college graduate, Gerry hadn't really focused on anything but sports and perhaps being on TV or radio. There are many athletes, both male and female, like Gerry who have extraordinary athletic abilities, but really are not equipped to do much else. In high school, there were many kids who hung around Gerry to bask in the limelight surrounding a famous athlete. There were a few who were not a good influence, but after some parental guidance and advice from me, Gerry straightened up. Gerry could be easily influenced, both in a good and a bad way, so I watched carefully who hung around when training was in progress.

When we came to Forest Lakes to make arrangements for the Bicentennial Race, one of the first people we met was Lu Fox. Lu and Gerry had known each other since childhood. Lu had opened a sports bar and was very successful. It was the place that everyone went to, especially when there were any big sporting events. Everyone knew there was some betting there, but it was just social betting as far as I knew. Lu and Gerry spent a lot of time together during our visit. They even walked the course, especially the Bermuda Triangle. Both agreed that this was going to be fun and add a bit of mystery to the race. Lu even volunteered to be one of the spotters in that section of the race. Harry Eagleton was going to be the other one. The morning of the race, Harry called in and said he was running a fever and wouldn't be able to be a spotter. I don't think anyone took his place. Why would they? This was only a race for fun—nothing official.

The day of the race, I waited at the finish line, fully expecting Gerry to come out first. When Jamie first appeared, I panicked. I thought that maybe Gerry had been hurt. Last year, Gerry missed a big race because of a twisted ankle. My greatest fear was that Gerry would be hurt in a contest such as this. Many athletes don't compete in exhibition games because of this reason. There's always the risk of getting hurt in regular competition, but to get hurt in some unofficial event is really devastating.

At any rate, Gerry finally came out in the clearing, running at record speed but it was too late. Jamie had crossed the finish line first. At first Gerry appeared upset, but then I guess my emphasis on good sportsmanship took hold and Gerry smiled and put an arm around Jamie and handed over the trophy.

I heard the allegations about Lu Fox and Gerry and find them unbelievable. I really don't know Lu that well, but I do know Gerry. Although Gerry likes to go along with his friends, he never would put a future in athletics, and perhaps a career based on it, in jeopardy. As for betting, I don't even think Gerry would know how, never having been around an atmosphere where betting is common.

_____
Affiant

SWORN TO AND SUBSCRIBED before me this _____ day of
_____ in this year_____

_____
NOTARY PUBLIC
State of _____
My Commission Expires: _____

IN THE CIRCUIT COURT OF THE EIGHTH JUDICIAL CIRCUIT, IN AND FOR JOHNSON COUNTY, _____

THE STATE OF _____
 Plaintiff
-v-   CASE NO.: 12-345-CF
GERRY RABBITT and
LU FOX
Defendants

GENERAL AFFIDAVIT

Drew Walters, being first duly sworn according to law, deposes and says that:

I've lived in Forest Lakes for about 10 years and my family loves it here. I really don't know Jamie Tortoise or Gerry Rabbitt, but I have heard townspeople talk about them. Can't say I've ever heard anything negative about either of them. Everyone is really proud of them. You could tell by that big sign as you came into town "Home of Champions—Jamie Tortoise and Gerry Rabbitt."

When Sal Barney suggested that we ask them to participate in our celebration, everyone thought it was a good idea. When the idea of the race came up, some of us were skeptical. How could we have a real race between two runners who had such different styles? Just when we were about to discard the race idea, Lu Fox came in with a plan to make it a "mystery race," suggesting that we have part of the race that spectators couldn't see on a path too narrow for cars to follow. We would have a spotter or two on foot instead of the cars, communicating by cell phone and reporting if anything should happen—you know, a runner tripping or something. We could call it the "Bermuda Triangle." There was even a map of how it could be done. We discussed it and said that even if the race was a "sure thing" for Rabbitt, this would lend an air of excitement, especially for the kids who are always intrigued by the stories of planes and boats disappearing in the Bermuda Triangle.

I volunteered to drive the car that would lead the runner to the finish line. I was to wait until I saw the leader come out of the clearing and guide the runner to the finish line. You can imagine how surprised I was to see Jamie. I was actually looking for Gerry in my rear view mirror. At first, I didn't see Jamie—he is so much shorter than Gerry. As I crossed the finish line with Jamie right behind me, Gerry suddenly came racing furiously and missed winning the race by about 2 feet. Everyone was cheering wildly. At first, Gerry seemed angry, but then smiling, he helped hand the trophy to Jamie.

I had heard earlier that there was betting on the race, but I didn't think anything of it. It couldn't be anything big. I often went to Lu's Place to watch big football or basketball games. There was always some friendly betting going on. I admit I even bet a few bucks myself. I didn't see much sense in betting on this race, because it was a sure thing that Gerry was going to win. After all, here's an Olympic runner who is used to competing in races. Jamie was a baseball player who used cunning rather than speed to steal bases.

Then, Sal Barney told me that we should look into possible irregularities because several people had complained that the race may have been rigged. Apparently these were people who had bet heavily on Gerry. Sal was devastated, having spent so much time preparing for this event. We discussed it and decided to call in Sam Hawkins, the police chief. Since Sam has been chief, our town has earned a reputation of having a police force that is fair and thorough. We felt that Sam would get to the bottom of this if there was any illegal activities.

I find it hard to believe that Gerry would do anything illegal. Everyone knew that the state had denied permission to have legal betting on the race. Gerry has so much invested in a sports career. You've seen so many of these ex-Olympic athletes who have gone onto bigger careers on TV as sports commentators. Gerry would be a natural.

Lu's a real hard worker who has built that sports bar into one of the major places to view sports in the state. Pictures and other sports items (some autographed by famous athletes) are hung on all the walls, and Lu's constantly changing them so the place is always interesting.

_____

Affiant

SWORN TO AND SUBSCRIBED before me this _____ day of
_____ in this year _____

_____

NOTARY PUBLIC
State of _____
My Commission Expires: _____

IN THE CIRCUIT COURT OF THE EIGHTH JUDICIAL CIRCUIT,
IN AND FOR JOHNSON COUNTY, _____

THE STATE OF _____
  Plaintiff
-v-   CASE NO.: 12-345-CF
GERRY RABBITT and
LU FOX
Defendants

JURY BALLOT

VERDICT

Please circle your choice:
To the charge: Influencing the outcome of a sporting event, Gerry Rabbitt is

           GUILTY   NOT GUILTY

SO SAY WE ALL:

    DATED in Forest Lakes, Johnson County, _____, this ____
                   day of _____ in the year _____

                                 _____
                                       Foreperson

IN THE CIRCUIT COURT OF THE EIGHTH JUDICIAL CIRCUIT, IN AND FOR JOHNSON COUNTY, _____

THE STATE OF _____
 Plaintiff
-v-
GERRY RABBITT and
LU FOX
Defendants

CASE NO.: 12-345-CF

JURY BALLOT

VERDICT

Please circle your choice:
To the charge: Influencing the outcome of a sporting event, Lu Fox is

GUILTY   NOT GUILTY

To the charge: Illegal betting, Lu Fox is

GUILTY   NOT GUILTY

SO SAY WE ALL:

DATED in Forest Lakes, Johnson County, _____, this ____
day of _____ in the year _____

_____
Foreperson

United States v. Susan B. Anthony

The following trial may be used to help students understand how the U.S. Constitution is interpreted. We often hear members of the U.S. Supreme Court state that their decisions are based on the wording of the Constitution. This trial is an example of how differing interpretations of a few words in the Constitution led to a historic trial.

Many students and adults are not aware of the fact that women did not obtain the right to vote until 1920. (You may want to share Table 3, a timeline of the events in the Women's Rights Movement, with your students). This trial, while focusing on the women's suffrage movement, is also an illustration of the difference between rights granted by states and the federal government. At issue in the trial is not only granting women the right to vote, but also the right of the federal government to supersede the states' rights. The signers of the U.S. Constitution had intended that each individual state should have the right to decide who would be allowed to vote. Passing an amendment transferring this right to the federal government was a major change.

Background Information

The Constitution of the United States of America was ratified in Philadelphia, PA, in 1787. In the Constitution, the matter of voting qualifications was left to be decided by the individual states. New Jersey was the only state that didn't require the voters to be male. (This was later rescinded.)

In the mid 1800s, women became active in many causes, such as better education for girls, equal pay and freedom for women to pursue careers of their

Table 3.
Timeline of the Women's Rights Movement

1787: The Constitution of the United States is ratified. It leaves the matter of voter qualifications up to the individual states. New Jersey is the only state that permits women to vote. In 1807, women in New Jersey lose this right.

1848: The Women's Suffrage Movement was originally part of a joint effort to end both slavery and to extend rights for women and Black citizens. Because women had been denied entrance to an abolitionist convention, it was decided to hold the first Women's Rights Convention in 1848. Lucretia Mott and Elizabeth Cady Stanton presided over the meeting.

1866: The American Equal Rights Association was founded. Its goal was to secure civil rights for all Americans regardless of race, color, or gender. Lucretia Mott was president.

1866: Elizabeth Cady Stanton tests an obscure 1788 law that allows women to run for office by running for Congress. She received only 24 of the 121,000 votes cast.

1867: Stanton, Lucy Stanton, and Susan B. Anthony attend the New York Constitutional Convention to request an amendment guaranteeing women's suffrage in the newly revised state constitution. The appeal failed.

1868: The 14th Amendment became part of the U.S. Constitution. The second section is written to encourage states to give the vote to Black males.

1869: Women's Suffrage Law passed in the Territory of Wyoming.

1870: The 15th Amendment is ratified. It states that the right to vote of citizens of the United States shall not be denied because of race, color, or previous condition of servitude. This allows former Black male slaves to vote, but still does not give the right to vote to women.

1872: Susan B. Anthony and 15 women register and vote in Rochester, NY, in the November presidential election. They and the officials who allowed them to register and vote are later arrested for the crime of "illegal voting."

1873: Susan B. Anthony and others involved in the "illegal registration and voting" in the 1872 presidential election are tried in Canandaigua, NY. The presiding judge directed the jury to render a guilty verdict.

1890: The National Women Suffrage Association and the American Women Suffrage Association merge to form the National American Woman Suffrage

Table 3 continued.

Association (NAWSA). This is now the movement's organization. NAWSA wages state-by-state campaigns to obtain voting rights for women.

1893: Colorado is the first state to adopt an amendment granting women the right to vote. Utah and Idaho follow suit in 1896, with Washington State following in 1910, California in 1911, Oregon, Kansas, and Arizona in 1912, Alaska and Illinois in 1913, Montana and Nevada in 1914, New York in 1917, Michigan, South Dakota, and Oklahoma in 1918.

1920: The 19th Amendment to the U.S. Constitution is ratified, giving women the right to vote.

choice, property rights, and custody of children. They were also active in anti-slavery (abolition) and temperance movements. It soon was realized that without the right to vote, women had little influence in any of these causes.

In July 1868, the 14th Amendment became part of the U.S. Constitution. It read:

> Section 2. Representatives shall be apportioned among the several States according to their respective numbers, counting the whole number of persons in each State, excluding Indians not taxed. But when the right to vote at any election for the choice of Electors for President and Vice President of the United States, Representatives in Congress, the executive and judicial officers of a State or the member of the legislature thereof, is denied to any of *the male inhabitants* of such State, being twenty-one years of age, and citizens of the United States, or in any way abridged except for participation in rebellion or other crime, the basis of representation therein shall be reduced to the proportion which the number of such *male citizens* shall bear to the whole number of *male citizens* twenty-one years of age in such State. (Emphasis added.)

The purpose of this amendment was to give the right to vote to *Black males.* This was the first time that the word *male* had been written in the Constitution.

Supporters of women's rights pointed out that citizenship of females seemed to now be in doubt. Women did not have the right of property ownership or child custody.

The husband not only owned all of the property, but if a woman worked, all of her wages belonged to her husband. Women did not have rights equal to men in many areas. The supporters pointed out that Section 1 of the 14th Amendment read:

> Section 1. *All persons* born or naturalized in the United States and subject to the jurisdiction thereof are citizens of the United States and of the state wherein they reside. No state shall make or enforce any law which shall abridge the privileges or immunities of citizens of the United States; nor shall any State deprive *any person* of life, liberty or property, without due process of law; nor deny to *any person* within its jurisdiction the equal protection of the laws. (Emphasis added.)

On November 5, 1872, Susan B. Anthony and 14 other women registered and then voted in the presidential election in Rochester, NY. At this time, each state had its own constitution that could decide who was eligible to vote. The U.S. Government deferred this decision to the states. In 1821, New York State's second Constitutional Convention extended voting rights to male citizens over 21 who held property, performed military service, or worked on highways. It did not grant women the right to vote.

On November 28, Anthony and the 14 women and the male inspectors who had registered them were arrested. Bail was set at $500 each and all but Anthony elected to pay it. Her bail was reset at $1,000. She still refused to pay it, and her attorney, Henry R. Selden, elected to pay it rather than see her go to jail.

The original trial of Susan B. Anthony and her codefendants was scheduled for May 13, 1873, in Monroe County, NY. Prior to the trial, Anthony traveled to all 29 postal districts in the county to tell her side of the story. It was felt that she had prejudiced any possible jury in Monroe County and the trial was rescheduled for June 17, 1873 and moved to Canandaigua, in Ontario County, NY. Anthony was charged with "unlawful voting."

The prosecution at this trial used as a basis for its charges the wording of Section 2 of the 14th Amendment of the U.S. Constitution. The attorneys for Susan B.

Anthony and her codefendants based their defense on Section 1 of the 14th Amendment.

U.S. District Judge Ward Hunt presided. Chief lawyers for the defendant were Henry R. Selden and John Van Voorhis. The Chief prosecutor was Richard Crowley.

Although the trial was before a jury, Judge Hunt read the following statement, directing the jury to deliver a guilty verdict:

> The right of voting, or the privilege of voting is a right or privilege arising under the Constitution of the State, and not of the United States. . . . If the State of New York should provide that no person should vote until he had reached the age of 31 years, or after he reached the age of 50. . . . I do not know how it could be held to be a violation of any right derived or held under the Constitution of the United States.

Judge Hunt refused Selden's request to poll the jury and did not allow Susan B. Anthony to make a final statement. He ordered her to pay a fine of $100 and the costs of prosecution. She replied, "May it please your honor, I will never pay a dollar of your unjust penalty. . . . Resistance to tyranny is obedience to God." Hunt released her, saying, "Madam, the Court will not order you to stand committed until the fine is paid."

Definitions

Abolition—abolishing or ending slavery.
Civil disobedience—refusal to obey government demands or commands in a nonviolent manner.
Indict—to charge with a fault or offense.
Suffrage—the right of voting.
Suffragette—woman who advocates suffrage for women.
Temperance—moderation in or abstinence from the use of intoxicating drink.

Exhibits/Materials

- Copy of the U.S. Constitution

Trial Participants

In keeping with the laws in effect at this time, women were not allowed to serve on juries or become attorneys. If female students serve in these roles, they should take the identity of a male attorney or male jury member and dress accordingly. For mock trial purposes, Susan B. Anthony and Rhoda DeGarmo will be allowed to testify. It is doubtful that they would have been allowed to take the stand in 1875.

Prosecution: Attorneys, Richard Crowley, Beverly W. Jones, Sylvester Lewis
Defense: Attorneys, Susan B. Anthony, Henry Selden, Rhoda DeGarmo

Formulating Questions for Direct and Cross-Examination

The mock trials in this book have been designed to allow for no clear-cut solutions. It is up to the attorneys to explore the affidavits of the opposition for weaknesses and inconsistencies. It is very important that all affidavits be looked at in this way, so that students can prepare for cross-examination. Students should be especially careful to analyze the affidavit of each witness to determine what information is factual and which is opinion. *Opinions are only admissible as testimony if offered by an expert witness.* An example would be a DNA expert who could give an opinion as to whether physical evidence at a crime scene matched the DNA pattern of a person accused of the crime.

I have found it best to allow the students to explore their own ideas first. Then, ask them specific questions and have them suggest possible ways that both the prosecution and defense might approach each question. By doing this, the students come to understand that they must look at all aspects of the case from both sides. The sample question below gives possible approaches by the prosecution and the defense.

> *Example:* Why did inspectors at the voting place accept the written opinion of a Missouri lawyer (Francis Minor) that Miss Anthony showed them as proof that women should be allowed to vote?
> *Prosecution:* They didn't understand the law and were afraid of a lawsuit.
> *Defense:* They believed that the evidence Miss Anthony presented was valid and proof that women should be allowed to vote:

You may want to use some of the following questions as guidelines in helping students prepare direct and cross-examination. (Remind the students that an attorney never asks a question on cross-examination unless he or she knows the answer the witness will give.)

- If Susan B. Anthony and the other women knew that the states granted the right to vote, why did they use the U.S. Constitution as a reference for their attempt to vote?
- If Susan B. Anthony knew that the U.S. Constitution gives the individual states the right to decide who will vote, why didn't she and her group mount a challenge at the state level? They had been successful in having the Married Women's Property Bill pass.
- As U.S. citizens, why didn't any of the men waiting to vote speak up and prevent Miss Anthony and her group from breaking the law?
- Did affiliation with individual political parties (Democratic or Republican) play any part in what happened on Election Day?
- Did the actions of Miss Anthony and her group help or hinder the Women's Rights Movement?

Trial Documents

The pages that follow include a statement of facts about the trial, affidavits from each witness, and forms for the jury to determine guilt or innocence. These forms are reproducible and should be given to all students helping to prepare for the trial.

Bibliography

The following sources were some of those used in preparing this mock trial. Direct quotations found in the mock trial appear in standard accounts of the times.

- Bjornlund, L. (2003). *Women of the suffrage movement.* San Diego, CA: Lucent Books.
- Dumbeck, K. (2001). *Leaders of women's suffrage.* San Diego, CA: Lucent Books.
- http://www.fjc.gov/history/anthony.nsf/autoframe
- http://www.law.umkc.edu/faculty/projects/ftrials/anthony/sbahome.html

Note: Because of the abundance of Internet sources for information about this trial, it is preferable to limit students to the use of information contained in the statement of facts and affidavits of the individual witnesses. This will result in a trial that can be more easily controlled.

IN THE UNITED STATES CIRCUIT COURT,
NORTHERN DISTRICT OF NEW YORK,
MONROE COUNTY, NEW YORK

CASE NO. 1873-32 PC

THE UNITED STATES OF AMERICA
    Plaintiff
-v-
SUSAN B. ANTHONY
    Defendant

STATEMENT OF FACTS

(Modified for mock trial purposes)

This case was reversed and remanded for a new trial after a *hypothetical appeal* to the Supreme Court of the United States challenged the verdict of guilt rendered on June 18, 1873, against the defendant, Susan B. Anthony, and 14 other women. (The verdict of the June 18, 1873 trial stood and was not appealed. *For purposes of this mock trial, we are assuming that there was an appeal to the United States Supreme Court. As a result of this hypothetical appeal, a new trial was granted.* This mock trial is based on what might have happened had Anthony been given a new trial after an appeal. The information concerning the appeal is not factual; all other facts are true to the events of the time.)

The Supreme Court ruled that the defendants did not receive a fair trial before an impartial jury and found that the jury had not been allowed to properly deliberate because they were ordered by presiding U.S. District Court Judge Ward Hunt to find the defendants guilty.

The trial was held on June 17, 1873, and the jury found the defendants guilty of unlawful voting, a federal criminal offense. Susan B. Anthony was the only defendant who appealed the verdict. The Court of Appeals for the Second Circuit affirmed the trial court verdict and an appeal to the United States Supreme Court followed. The Court agreed to review the case. After appellate briefs were filed and oral arguments heard, the Supreme Court ruled that special jury instructions prepared by U.S. District Court Judge Ward Hunt were prejudicial and unfair. As a result, the defendants did not "enjoy the right to a speedy and public trial by an *impartial jury* of the State and district wherein the crime shall have been committed" (emphasis added) in violation of the Sixth Amendment to the United States Constitution. The Supreme Court directed that the defendant, Susan B. Anthony, be granted a new trial.

The circumstances that led to the arrest of Susan B. Anthony and her codefendants are as follows:

Susan B. Anthony and 14 other women registered and then voted in the presidential election on November 5, 1872. At this time, each state had its own constitution, designating those who were eligible to vote. The federal government deferred to the states on this issue. On November 28, 1872, Anthony, 14 other women, and the male inspectors who had registered them were arrested and charged with the federal offense of unlawful voting. Bail was set at $500 for each defendant and all but Anthony decided to pay it. Her bail was then increased to $1,000. She still refused to pay and her attorney, Henry R. Selden, posted bond rather than have her go to jail.

The prosecution used as a basis for the charges the wording of Section 2 of the 14th Amendment, which became part of the U.S. Constitution in July 1868. The purpose of this amendment was to give the right to vote to *Black males*. This was the first time that the word male had been written in the Constitution. Section 2 reads:

> Representatives shall be apportioned among the several States according to their respective numbers, counting the whole number of persons in each State, excluding Indians not taxed. But when the right to vote at any election for the choice of electors for President and Vice President of the United States, Representatives in Congress, the executive and judicial officers of a State or the member of the legislature thereof, is denied to any of the *male inhabitants* of such State, being twenty-one years of age, and citizens of the United States, or in any way abridged except for participation in rebellion or other crime, the basis of representation therein shall be reduced to the proportion which the number of such *male citizens* shall bear to the whole number of *male citizens* twenty-one years of age in such State. (emphasis added)

Supporters of women's rights pointed out that citizenship of females seemed to now be in doubt. Women did not have rights of property ownership or child custody. The husband not only owned all property but if a woman worked, all of her wages belonged to her husband. Women did not have rights equal to men in many areas. The supporters pointed out that Section I of the 14th Amendment stated:

> *All persons* born or naturalized in the United States and subject to the jurisdiction thereof are citizens of the United States and of the state wherein they reside. No state shall make or enforce any law which shall abridge the privileges or immunities of citizens of the United States; nor shall any State deprive *any person* of life, liberty or property, without due process of law; nor deny to *any person* within its jurisdiction the equal protection of the laws. (emphasis added)

The original trial of Susan B. Anthony and her codefendants was scheduled for May 13, 1873, in Monroe County, NY. Prior to the trial, Anthony traveled to all 29 postal districts in the county to tell her side of the story. The determination was made that she had prejudiced potential jurors in Monroe County and the trial was rescheduled for July 17, 1873. A change of venue moved the case to Canandaigua in Ontario County, NY. U.S. District Judge Ward Hunt presided. Defense attorneys Henry R. Selden and John Van Voorhis represented the defendants. Chief prosecutor was Richard Crowley, who charged the defendants with the criminal offense of unlawful voting.

The jury found the defendants guilty of the crimes charged. However, even though this was a trial before a jury, as opposed to a bench trial where the judge is the trier of fact, Judge Hunt prepared special jury instructions and read the following statement, directing the jury to deliver a verdict of guilt.

> The right of voting, or the privilege of voting is a right or privilege arising under the Constitution of the State, and not of the United States. . . . If the State of New York should provide that no person should vote until he had reached the age of 31 years, or after he reached the age of 50. . . . I do not know how it could be held to be a violation of any right derived or held under the Constitution of the United States.

Judge Hunt refused to allow Susan B. Anthony or any of the other defendants to make closing arguments and refused defense attorney Selden's request to poll the jury after they rendered the verdicts of guilt. The trial court ordered Anthony to pay a fine of $100 and the costs of prosecution. She replied: "May it please your honor, I will never pay a dollar of your unjust penalty. . . . Resistance to tyranny is obedience to God." However, Judge Hunt refused to order her into custody, saying "Madam, the Court will not order you to stand committed until the fine is paid."

The purpose of the new trial in this case is to have fair and just proceedings whereby the defendant, Susan B. Anthony, will be judged by a jury who will render the final verdict based on the evidence presented and the amendments to the U.S. Constitution in effect in 1874. Based on the ruling by the United States Supreme Court, the trial judge is prohibited from reading his prior special jury instructions, which had been found to be unconstitutional in that he directed a verdict for the prosecution. It is the sole province of the jury to deliver a verdict as to the charges against the defendant.

IN THE UNITED STATES CIRCUIT COURT,
NORTHERN DISTRICT OF NEW YORK,
MONROE COUNTY, NEW YORK

CASE NO. 1873-32 PC

THE UNITED STATES OF AMERICA
    Plaintiff
-v-
SUSAN B. ANTHONY
    Defendant

GENERAL AFFIDAVIT

Richard Crowley, being first duly sworn according to law, deposes and says that:

I have been the U.S. attorney for the Northern District of New York since March 1871, when I was appointed to that position by President Ulysses S. Grant. I began practicing law in Lockport in 1860. Then I was city attorney for 2 years and a state senator for 4 years. During this time, I received the support of U.S. Senator Roscoe Conklin.

When Susan B. Anthony and the other defendants were charged, I oversaw their arrest, examination, and ultimately her indictment. I arranged the transfer from the district to the circuit court and was lead attorney for the government in her trial.

Miss Anthony claims that she had the right to vote on the basis of the 14th Amendment. Section 1 of this amendment has no bearing on this case. If you read it carefully, it states:

> No State shall make or enforce any law which shall abridge the privileges or immunities of citizens of the United States; nor shall any State deprive any person of life, liberty, or property, without due process of law; nor deny to any person within its jurisdiction the equal protection of the law.

Nothing is mentioned about the right to vote. Section 2 not only recognizes the right of states to abridge voting rights but also approved restrictions based on sex and age. It did not prohibit states from limiting the votes to males. The 14th Amendment protected voting rights only with respect to race, color, or previous condition of servitude.

Miss Anthony may claim that she did not "knowingly" commit a crime; however there were numerous ways that she could have known that she didn't have the right to vote. For instance, women suffragists had written a petition to the House Committee on the Judiciary giving their interpretation of the constitutional amendments. Congressman John Bingham of that committee wrote a response rejecting their interpretation.

Miss Anthony further believes that the right to vote is natural for all citizens. It is not. It is granted by law. If the states gave the rights to all citizens, there would be no way that the mentally ill or children could be barred from voting. There must be specific limitations on who can vote.

Miss Anthony claimed she acted on the advice of counsel and then she decided to vote. In truth when she had gone to her attorney, Henry Selden, for advice, she had already decided that she was going to vote. She did not act in good faith.

We don't claim that Miss Anthony is of that class of people who go about "repeating." We don't claim that she went from place to place for the purpose of offering her vote. But we do claim that upon the 5th of November, 1872, she voted, and whether she believed that she had a right to vote or not, it being a question of law, that she is within the Statute.*

We did concede that on the 5th day of November, 1872, Miss Susan B. Anthony is a woman.

*Exact words of Lead Prosecution Counsel, Richard Crowley, in the trial of Susan B. Anthony which was held on June 17 and 18, 1873 before Honorable Judge Ward Hunt, and a jury in Canandaigua, NY.

_____
                                                          Affiant

SWORN TO AND SUBSCRIBED before me this _____
            ____day of_____ in the year 1875

_____
                                      NOTARY PUBLIC
                                      State of New York

                          My Commission Expires: _____

IN THE UNITED STATES CIRCUIT COURT,
NORTHERN DISTRICT OF NEW YORK,
MONROE COUNTY, NEW YORK

CASE NO. 1873-32 PC

THE UNITED STATES OF AMERICA
    Plaintiff
-v-
SUSAN B. ANTHONY
    Defendant

GENERAL AFFIDAVIT

<u>Beverly W. Jones</u>, being first duly sworn according to law, deposes and
says that:

My name is Beverly W. Jones and I live in the Eighth Ward in
Rochester, NY. Many people confuse my name with that of a woman's, but
when they see me at the voting place, helping men to vote, they know that I
am a man, because no woman has that right.

I was one of the inspectors at the polling place in Rochester. There are
two election districts in the Eighth Ward, and I was an inspector in the
First District. Miss Susan B. Anthony and some other women came in and
wanted to register to vote on November 1, 1872. Another inspector, Edwin
Marsh, and I refused to let them do so.

We didn't want to let them register and I pointed out that it was against
the law of the State of New York. Miss Anthony showed us a written
opinion by Francis Minor, a lawyer from Missouri, that said that Section 1
of the 14th Amendment of the U.S. Constitution stated:

All persons born or naturalized in the United States, and subject to
the jurisdiction thereof, are citizens of the United States and of the
state wherein they reside. No state shall make or enforce any law
which shall abridge the privileges or immunities of citizens of the
United States. (emphasis added)

She said that if we turned them away, there would be a lawsuit against
us. Section 1 did say "all persons." To me, that meant women, too. The
other registrars and I discussed this and we agreed, not very strongly,
that while New York State law said women could not vote, the U.S.
Constitution said they could. We reluctantly let them register. Many other
women then heard about the incident and by the end of the day, we had 50
women come into register. After they left, we put their registrations aside.

We thought that the women had achieved what they wanted to do—register to vote.

Imagine our surprise when bright and early on the morning of Election Day, November 5, a group of about 15 women marched in. They were arm in arm to show that they were united, I guess. Miss Anthony stepped forward and said they had come to vote. In addition to Miss Anthony were her three sisters. Remembering the words of the U.S. Constitution's 14th Amendment that Miss Anthony had showed us, we let the women vote all of the tickets.

There were four tickets to be voted on that day: the Electoral ticket (for president), Congressional ticket, State ticket, and Assembly ticket. Each ticket had a separate box and the women's votes were deposited in these boxes.

I must say the men waiting to vote either thought it was amusing or said some ugly things to the women about staying home where they belonged. The women probably thought they were voting for president—didn't realize that voters only vote for electors and these electors really elect the president. The only candidates for federal office they could vote for were for members of Congress.

Everything seemed to be going well and the other inspectors and I heard nothing more about allowing the women to vote. We thought the whole incident had been forgotten. Then, on November 18, a U.S. Marshall came and served me with an arrest warrant. He told me that Miss Anthony, some of the women and the other inspectors had also received warrants. Miss Anthony was charged with "knowingly, wrongfully and unlawfully voting for a representative to the Congress of the United States." The other registrars and I were charged with helping her to do so.

Our bail was set at $500 each. We paid it, but Miss Anthony refused to pay hers. She would have been sent to jail, but her attorney, Henry Selden, paid the bail money. He didn't want to have a lady he respected sent to jail. I must agree with him. Susan B. Anthony is quite an intelligent lady and she fights for what she believes in; however, the U.S. Constitution is the law of the land and has served us well for many years. We can't just take the words and twist them to meet our own needs. I later read Section 2 of the 14th Amendment to the Constitution. It clearly specifies "male citizens" and to me, that means women do not have the right to vote, no matter what Section 1 says.

When Justice Ward Hunt directed a guilty verdict for Miss Anthony, I must say I was surprised, but I don't think it would have made a difference if he had polled the jury. Miss Anthony and the other ladies who had registered and voted had done so illegally. The U.S. Constitution specifically states that males are allowed to vote. It does not give women the right to vote. The laws of the State of New York which governs the specifics about who can vote, does not give women the right to vote either.

Clearly, Miss Anthony and any other women who voted on Election Day, November 5, broke the law.

_____
Affiant

SWORN TO AND SUBSCRIBED before me this _____
_____ day of _____ in the year 1875

_____
NOTARY PUBLIC
State of New York

My Commission Expires: _____

IN THE UNITED STATES CIRCUIT COURT,
NORTHERN DISTRICT OF NEW YORK,
MONROE COUNTY, NEW YORK

CASE NO. 1873-32 PC

THE UNITED STATES OF AMERICA
    Plaintiff
-v-
SUSAN B. ANTHONY
    Defendant

GENERAL AFFIDAVIT

<u>Sylvester Lewis</u>, being first duly sworn according to law, deposes and says that:

I live in the Eighth Ward in Rochester, and I have a salt manufacturing business. At the time of the election in November of 1872, I was hired by the Democratic Party to get out the vote—you know, make sure we got all of the legal voters to the polls. If anyone came in to vote and I didn't think they had the right to vote, it was my job to challenge them.

When Susan B. Anthony and her group came in to vote, I knew that women couldn't vote, so I challenged her. She said something about the 14th Amendment giving her the right to vote. When she said this, I was bound by law to have her swear an oath that she was qualified to vote and had not accepted a bribe.

I felt it was my job to challenge any voter that was questionable. I was upholding the constitutions of the United States of America and the State of New York. These documents were written by men whose superior intelligence gave them the ability to write such laws. No woman is capable of being able to do this.

I will say that women are far superior when it comes to running a household and taking care of domestic affairs. Frankly, I don't see where they have the time to pay attention to matters that are important to our society, both nationally and internationally. Men and women are different not only physically, but mentally and emotionally. Men can devote their entire time to deciding the laws of the land. Women are not qualified intellectually to handle such matters. It is a well-known fact that the female of the human species is inferior to the male.

If they want to make their opinions known, married women can let their husbands know if they have any viewpoints on specific topics. Unmarried women, many of whom are teachers, can impart their knowledge on the young men in their classroom. These youngsters can then take this information and form their own enlightened opinions.

I want to make clear my opposition to male advocates of woman suffrage: *Let them choose for themselves a legal representative whose duty it shall be to assist in making the laws and grappling with the stern realities of life, while she contents herself to attend to the domestic affairs of her household.*

When Justice Ward Hunt directed a guilty verdict in the first trial, he made a big mistake by not polling the jury. I'm sure if they had been polled, there would have been a unanimous verdict of guilty, and we would not be dealing with this second trial.

I may as well clear up some rumors that have been spread. Someone said that I had urged a woman from a Democratic household to register to vote. They also said that I had registered some Irish women and paid them to vote Democratic. Apparently, some people do not recognize humor when they hear it. I was just having a good time and joking a bit. I would never register any woman to vote. I challenged Susan B. Anthony and her group, didn't I? Why, if it hadn't been for me, no one would have questioned her right to vote. As for paying some Irish women to register and to vote, that is outrageous. Buying votes is a crime—whether the voter is male of female.

I am an upstanding businessman in our community and I would do nothing to jeopardize my reputation.

* This is an exact quote from Sylvester Lewis.

_____
                                        Affiant

SWORN TO AND SUBSCRIBED before me this _____
_____day of_____ in the year 1875

_____
                        NOTARY PUBLIC
                        State of New York

                        My Commission Expires: _____

IN THE UNITED STATES CIRCUIT COURT,
NORTHERN DISTRICT OF NEW YORK,
MONROE COUNTY, NEW YORK

CASE NO. 1873-32 PC

THE UNITED STATES OF AMERICA
    Plaintiff
-v-
SUSAN B. ANTHONY
    Defendant

GENERAL AFFIDAVIT

<u>Susan B. Anthony</u>, being first duly sworn according to law, deposes and says that:

I was brought up in a Quaker community. The Quakers allowed women to speak freely at their meetings. It was usually about church business, but still we had our say. I was always a good student, but my father felt that I really didn't need to know subjects including science and math. It was felt that all a woman needed to know in arithmetic was the basics so she could weigh butter and count eggs. As a result, instead of going to an academy where women could study all kinds of subjects, I had to go to a seminary for girls. As I grew older, my uncle came to my rescue. He must have realized my qualifications and potential and invited me to head the girl's department at Canajoharie Academy in New York

This was a real eye-opener. Not only did I live in an entirely different world than the one I knew as a child, but I learned more about the restrictions put on women by our legal system. At first, I must admit I did not think that women should have the right to vote. When I returned home to visit my family, I found that they had attended convention meetings in which Elizabeth Cady Stanton and Lucretia Mott had spoken. I had read a lot about both of them and agreed wholeheartedly with their ideas that girls should receive a better education and women should have equal pay and the ability to pursue careers of their choice. A woman should also have the right to own property and have custody of her children. The idea that a woman should have the right to vote seemed a bit far-fetched. My family convinced me that this was as much a right for women as any of the others.

I was already working for the abolition of slavery and temperance—the use of alcohol has caused so very many tragedies in the lives of families. Children have been particularly affected in this matter. I felt I really didn't have the time to work for women's votes. Then I realized that women *had* to have the right to vote if we were going to make any headway in other issues such as antislavery and temperance. Working for women to have the right to vote became my new mission. I traveled throughout the state of New York. The more I traveled, the more I witnessed women who not only were denied custody of their children but who also did not have the ability to sue for divorce. Because they couldn't control their own money, they were helpless. I witnessed women working hard day and night, only to have their husbands show up on payday to claim their wages. We had some measure of success in 1860 when Elizabeth Cady Stanton and I were able to get the Married Women's Property Bill passed in New York. This allowed a woman to own property, keep whatever money she had earned working, have joint custody of children with her husband, and many other rights. It was a huge victory for women.

In 1868, the 14th Amendment to the U.S. Constitution was passed. It stated that the right to vote could not be denied to any of the *male inhabitants* of each state who were 21 years old and citizens of the United States. This, in effect, gave the right to vote to *Black males*. This was wonderful. Ex-slaves would now enjoy the rights of citizenship; however, the amendment specified males and made no mention of the rights of women. One victory was won, but women were still being denied their rights.

The passing of that amendment spurred women into action. We pointed out that while Section 2 of the 14th Amendment gave the right to all males, Section 1 stated that "*all persons* born or naturalized in the United States . . . are citizens" (emphasis added). It further stated "nor shall any State deprive *any person* of life, liberty or property, without due process of law nor deny to *any person* within its jurisdiction the equal protection of the laws" (emphasis added). We believed that with these words, the Constitution of the land reaffirmed that women had the right to vote.

Before, women had worked tirelessly for abolition of slavery and temperance—now it was time for us to work for fundamental rights for ourselves. If we could get the right to vote, we would have a voice in our government and achieve so much more

We could talk all we wanted. We could hold conventions, but if we were to accomplish anything, we were going to have to take bold action. Our group discussed it and I finally convinced 15 of them to register on November 3, 1872, in Rochester, NY, for the presidential election to be held on November 5. I guess the men who helped us register either agreed with us or didn't think we would have the nerve to vote.

On Election Day, at 7 a.m., we arrived promptly at the voting place. My three sisters and I entered arm in arm to cast our ballots. The officials didn't fully understand what was going on and before they knew it, 17 women had actually voted!

We achieved what we had set out to do. Our voting gained national attention—some favorable, some not.

Then, on November 18, a U.S. Marshall came to arrest me. We were going to the police station. When we got on a streetcar, he expected me to pay my fare. Can you imagine that? Of course, I refused. He paid my fare.

I was charged with "knowingly, wrongfully and unlawfully voting for a representative to the Congress of the United States." The trial was originally scheduled for May 13, 1873, in Monroe County, NY. I knew the only way I had a chance was to let people know what had happened and why these women and I had taken such a drastic step. Before the trial, I went to all 29 postal districts in the county and pleaded our case.

When it was heard what I had done, it was decided that I had prejudiced any possible jury in Monroe County. The trial was moved to Canandaigua in Ontario County, NY, and rescheduled for June 17, 1873. U.S. District Judge Ward Hunt presided. After testimony was presented, he directed the jury to deliver a guilty verdict and refused to allow the jury to be polled. My attorney, Mr. Selden, and I felt that justice had not been served and decided to appeal. Fortunately, our request was granted and we will again have the opportunity to present our case.

So, here we are, ready to be tried before a male judge, male lawyers, and a male jury deciding the verdict. During my many speeches and visits with people throughout New York, I found many men who were open-minded and understood that our country would benefit by allowing women to vote. They realized that there are as many intelligent women as there are intelligent men in the United States. I hope that some of these open-minded, intelligent men are selected for the jury.

_____
                                Affiant

SWORN TO AND SUBSCRIBED before me this _____
_____day of_____ in the year 1875

_____
                   NOTARY PUBLIC
                   State of New York

                   My Commission Expires: _____

IN THE UNITED STATES CIRCUIT COURT,
NORTHERN DISTRICT OF NEW YORK,
MONROE COUNTY, NEW YORK

CASE NO. 1873-32 PC

THE UNITED STATES OF AMERICA
    Plaintiff
-v-
SUSAN B. ANTHONY
    Defendant

GENERAL AFFIDAVIT

Henry Selden,* being first duly sworn according to law, deposes and says that:

I've lived in the Rochester, NY, area all of my adult life. I was a State Reporter for the New York State Court of Appeals and helped establish the New York State Republican party in 1856. That year I became New York's first Republican Lieutenant Governor and held that position for 2 years. In 1862, I was appointed as an Associate Judge of the New York State Court of Appeals, I held this position until 1865 when I was elected to the New York State Legislature. In 1872, I decided I'd had enough of politics and returned to my law practice.

Susan B. Anthony came to me in early 1872 and wanted my opinion on whether or not she had legal grounds to vote. She had done extensive research. She was well prepared. I understand that many of the local lawyers would not take her case. My brother Samuel, who is also a lawyer, and I reviewed the materials she had and believed that she did indeed have the right to vote. Because of our advice, she and many other women registered and voted on Election Day, November 5, 1872. She and several other women and the male inspectors at the voting place were arrested for illegal voting

In my opinion, the idea that you can be charged with a crime on account of voting, or offering to vote, when you honestly believed yourself entitled to vote, is simply preposterous, whether your belief were right or wrong. However, the learned gentlemen engaged in this movement seem to suppose they can make a crime out of your honest deposit of your ballot, and perhaps they can find a respectable court of jury that will be of their opinion. If they do so I shall be greatly disappointed.

On January 21, 1873, we went before the U. S. District Judge and asked that the charges against Miss Anthony be discharged because they were illegal. Not only did the judge deny our request, he increased her bail. She refused to pay it. Rather than see this lady I respected so much go to jail, I paid the bond for her.

The 10th Amendment says, "The powers not delegated to the United States by the Constitution, nor prohibited by it in the States, are reserved to the States respectively, or to the people."

If we study the U.S. Constitution carefully, we can see that Section 1 of the 14th Amendment does indeed state "*All persons* born or naturalized in the United States and subject to the jurisdiction thereof, are citizens of the United States and the State wherein they reside" (emphasis added). Section 2 of the same amendment contradicts this when it refers to *male citizens* and their rights. How can we talk only about the rights of male citizens? Nowhere in the Constitution before this amendment was the term *male* used to describe citizens. This clearly is an attempt to assure that women were denied the right to vote.

There are three questions that should be discussed in this trial:

**1. Was the defendant legally entitled to vote at the election in question?
  2. If she was not entitled to vote, but believed that she was, and voted in good faith in that belief, did such voting constitute a crime under the statute before referred to?
  3. Did the defendant vote in good faith in that belief? **

*For our mock trial purposes, Mr. Selden will appear as a witness for the Defense (Susan B. Anthony). This will permit student attorneys to plan their own strategies and questions for the trial.
**These are the exact words used by Henry Selden when acting as defense attorney for Susan B. Anthony in the original trial.

_____
                                                Affiant

SWORN TO AND SUBSCRIBED before me this _____
          ____day of_____ in the year _1875_

_____
                                    NOTARY PUBLIC
                                    State of New York

                        My Commission Expires: _____

IN THE UNITED STATES CIRCUIT COURT,
NORTHERN DISTRICT OF NEW YORK,
MONROE COUNTY, NEW YORK

CASE NO. 1873-32 PC

THE UNITED STATES OF AMERICA
   Plaintiff
-v-
SUSAN B. ANTHONY
   Defendant

GENERAL AFFIDAVIT

Rhoda DeGarmo, being first duly sworn according to law, deposes and says that:

My husband, Elias, and I live in Gates, NY, and have been long-time neighbors of the Anthony family. I have known Susan since she was a little girl. I like to think that I have been a positive influence on her.

I was an early member of the Western New York Anti-Slavery Society. I joined in 1842, the year that it was formed, and have held several important positions with the organization. We did all we could to raise awareness of the evil of slavery. Each year, we held an Anti-Slavery Fair to raise funds to support the cause. Some people apparently weren't fully in favor of what we believed in. In 1849, we had a great feast and invited "all classes and colours" to sit down at one table. It created quite a controversy.

You may have heard of the Underground Railroad. I was part of that and we often opened our home to ex-slaves on their way to Canada. The Anthonys were also very sympathetic to this cause.

I was also very active in the temperance cause. Alcoholic liquors have caused so many problems in our society. The effect they have on the American family is terrible. Many a man under the influence of alcohol has neglected his wife and his family—not only denying them support, but in some cases causing physical harm. Alcohol has turned an otherwise loving family man into a horrible creature.

When dealing with temperance, it became apparent that women were denied their rights in so many areas, like our Negro brethren. They were sometimes like servants in their own homes. They couldn't own property, or have legal custody of their children. If they had jobs outside of the home, their husbands could claim their pay. It became apparent that the only way their plight might change would be if they had some say in the laws of our land. The only way they could do this was to have a say in who made these laws. Women needed the right to vote.

In 1848, a group of us formed one of the first groups to work for women's suffrage and women's rights. We had a convention in Rochester, NY, and the Arrangements Committee convinced Abigail Bush to preside. Some of the other women thought that this was "a most hazardous experiment," but Abigail performed her duties so well, their doubts were put to rest.

In another first, Elias and I witnessed the marriage of our daughter in a ceremony performed by Antoinette Brown. Antoinette was one of the first ordained women ministers of a recognized denomination in the United States.

So, you can imagine how excited I was when I heard that Susan B. Anthony was going to try to register to vote in the presidential election of 1872. The civil rights movement for women had come a long way and I wanted to be part of it. At 73, I had witnessed progress in so many areas and I wanted to be part of this historic event.

On November 1, a group of us, led by Miss Anthony, entered the voting headquarters in the Eighth Ward. The registrars looked up and seemed amused at our presence. When Susan announced that we were there to register, they told it this was not possible. Then, she brought out copies of the U.S. Constitution and showed them the amendments that she felt supported our right to vote. They still did not want to let us register, but when we announced we would sue if we were denied our right to vote according to the U.S. Constitution, they relented.

I guess they thought that was the end of it. When we arrived early on Election Day, November 5, to vote, they were aghast. A gentleman (and I use the term loosely) by the name of Sylvester Lewis challenged Susan and said she would have to swear an oath that she was legally entitled to vote. Having the words of the U.S. Constitution to back her up, she took the oath. When they asked me to swear an oath, I refused. I was brought up a Quaker. According to our beliefs, I insisted that the fact that I would simply tell the truth should be enough.

I dare say that any of the men present would have been very upset if they had been humiliated the way we were. But, as women, we were used to this and knew that if we were going to forge ahead, we had to endure such treatment. In my 73 years here on Earth, I have been treated this way many times. But, that is the price to pay if we are going to make progress for women's rights.

_____
Affiant

SWORN TO AND SUBSCRIBED before me this _____
_____day of_____ in the year 1875

_____
NOTARY PUBLIC
State of New York

My Commission Expires: _____

IN THE UNITED STATES
CIRCUIT COURT,
NORTHERN DISTRICT OF NEW YORK,
MONROE COUNTY, NEW YORK

CASE NO. 1873-32 PC

THE UNITED STATES OF AMERICA
    Plaintiff
-v-
SUSAN B. ANTHONY
    Defendant

JURY BALLOT

VERDICT

Please circle your choice:
To the charge: Unlawful voting, *Susan B. Anthony* is

GUILTY   NOT GUILTY

SO SAY WE ALL:

_____
                                   Affiant

SWORN TO AND SUBSCRIBED before me this _____
_____day of_____ in the year <u>1875</u>

_____
                 NOTARY PUBLIC
                 State of New York

My Commission Expires: _____

CHAPTER 6

Civil Trials

Civil cases are not involved with offenses against laws made by a governing body. They deal with private problems between individuals or corporations involving such matters as responsibility for an accident, failure to fulfill the terms of a contract, malpractice, or damages from libel. The public is usually not involved and each party in the suit engages an attorney to present evidence and question witnesses.

The object of a civil action in which the defendant is judged to be wrong is an attempt to restore the situation to what it would have been had no legal wrong been committed. In most instances the defendant is ordered to pay the wrong party a sum of money. Other types of rulings include an *injunction* ordering the defendant not to do something or a judgment restoring property to its rightful owner.

If the offense is especially serious, the plaintiff may ask for *punitive damages* to punish the defendant. The court may award these if it wishes to impress upon the public at large that such offenses will not be tolerated.

In civil cases, a decision may be decided by a judge or a jury. If a jury hears the case, the verdict need not be unanimous. In most states, four or five out of six jurors will determine the outcome. You might want to check your local courts and find what procedure they follow.

When considering the evidence, the jury must decide in whose favor the facts weigh most heavily. Unlike criminal trials, the jury need not render a verdict based upon the absence of a reasonable doubt. A *preponderance of evidence* decides the verdict.

The civil trials shown here deal with characters easily recognized by your students. The familiar facts have been enhanced to provide the material necessary for a mock trial. The two civil trials presented in this book include the following.

- In *Goldie Locks v. Jo Deer, Owner and Editor of the* Gumperville Gazette, Goldie Locks is a real estate agent who has been falsely accused of trespassing. She is suing Jo Deer as the editor of the *Gumperville Gazette* for a story that was printed before the editor fully checked the facts. Teachers: the names of the minor characters are ambiguous, allowing either male or female students to play the characters. You may change the pronouns on the affidavits if you choose to have a student of the gender opposite to what is mentioned play the role.

- In *Squanto Jones v. Myles Standish*, Jones is suing Standish for opening a restaurant, Pilgrim's Fare, that had a menu clearly based on the food served at Jones' Wampanoags' Restaurant. Jones claims his recipes were originals and that by serving foods clearly made using these recipes, Standish violated "trade secrets." Teachers: the names of some of the minor characters are ambiguous, allowing either male or female students to play the characters. You may change the pronouns on the affidavits if you choose to have a student of the gender opposite to what is mentioned play the role.

Goldie Locks v. Jo Deer,
Owner and Editor of the *Gumperville Gazette*

Background Information

The story of "Goldilocks and the Three Bears" takes on a modern twist with this mock trial. Set in the bucolic town of Gumperville, we find Buford and Beulah Bear and their daughter, Buttons, living the typical lives of country bears. Buford and Beulah are having difficulty making financial ends meet because of a poor berry crop, so they have come up with the idea of turning their cozy country home into a bed-and-breakfast. Many members of the bruin community have commented on how nicely Beulah has decorated the place and has even added her own touch with her own special oatmeal mix which she has had packaged to give to friends. Buford is a typical country husband who maintains the outside of the home beautifully. Both of them have close friends in the community.

One day, Buford went into downtown Gumperville and noticed a new office had opened. The sign in the window said "Goldie Locks Realty" and noted that the firm specialized in rental properties. Buford went in to talk to the proprietor, Goldie Locks. After discussing the bed-and-breakfast idea, he believed that Goldie Locks might be able to help him and Beulah get their new enterprise up and running. He invited her to come see their house. She accepted the invitation, but said she would call first.

On the morning of May 12, Goldie Locks awakened well before dawn. She had not slept well because the bed she had just purchased was very uncomfortable. She decided to go for a ride to look around the town because she had only been there a short time. She remembered Buford Bear and decided to ride past his house before calling him later in the day to make an appointment.

In the meantime, Buford, Beulah, and Buttons had arisen at the usual time and gone for their usual walk before breakfast—something they did faithfully each day, rain or shine.

When Goldie Locks arrived at their home, she was very impressed with its country charm. She decided to get out of her car and walk around to get a better look at the exterior. She noticed the front door was slightly open. She knocked on the door and called out to see if anyone was home. As she was waiting for a response, she peeked inside and saw the kitchen. She walked in a little bit to get a better look. The kitchen was large and roomy and on the table was an inviting wicker basket with assorted packages of premixed oatmeal bearing Beulah Bear's name. Still enthralled, Ms. Locks walked through the house, going from room to room. She felt that if she was going to advertise this as a bed-and-breakfast, she must investigate all aspects of the home. As she visited each bedroom, she sat on the bed. The Bears had been very thoughtful and had beds of varying degrees of firmness. One she found to be a bit too hard, another a bit too soft, and then in the third bedroom, she found one that was perfect. After she sat down, she decided to really test it and lie down. She was exhausted from not having a good night's rest and promptly fell asleep.

Suddenly, she was awakened by a police officer brandishing a gun. She tried to explain, but then a woman, later identified as Beulah Bear, began screaming. Buttons Bear and the Bears' neighbor, Robin Ursa, also were there, adding to the confusion. The officer, Cpl. Kim Doyle decided that the safest thing would be to take Goldie Locks to the station. She was read her rights and handcuffed. As she was being taken to the patrol car, Fran Statler, a reporter for the *Gumperville Gazette*, began taking pictures. Ms. Locks protested the photos being taken, but to no avail.

Shortly after Ms. Locks was taken into custody, Buford Bear arrived home. He and Beulah had argued about his wanting to buy a new Jack Stag Supermower, so she and Buttons had returned home without him. When Buford saw Ms. Locks car in the driveway, he asked where she was. When Beulah told him what had happened, he immediately went down to the police station to explain the situation. Goldie Locks was released.

Unfortunately, reporter Fran Statler had taken the story, complete with pictures, to the office of the *Gumperville Gazette.* When Jo Deer, the editor, heard what had happened, the story was immediately prepared for publication in that day's edition of the paper. Because there was no time for the pictures to be prepared, the readers were alerted that the following day's issue would carry the full story complete with photos. Later that afternoon, Goldie Locks saw the paper on the newsstand and went directly to the *Gazette's* office. She demanded a retraction, and Jo Deer, after checking with the police, assured her one would be forthcoming.

When several days passed without a notice in the paper, Ms. Locks again complained. As a result Jo Deer printed a retraction. Unfortunately it was on a page near the back of the paper. Ms. Locks claims that few people saw it and that she wants a retraction on the front page because that's where the original story was printed. She also wants possession of all prints and negatives to assure that the pictures never reach the public.

In addition, she is suing for damages to her reputation. As a result of the newspaper article, she claims she has lost business.

Definitions

Bed-and-breakfast—an inn offering lodging and breakfast.
Bruin—a bear.
Hare—a rabbit.
Hibernate—to pass the winter in a resting state.
Insomnia—inability to obtain adequate sleep.
Obituary—notice of a person's death.
Put to bed—to make the final preparations for printing (as a newspaper).
Warren—a place where rabbits are kept.

Exhibits

- Packets of Beulah Bear's special oatmeal (optional)
- May 12 edition of *Gumperville Gazette* (see Figure 7)
- May 17 edition of *Gumperville Gazette* (see Figure 8)

Trial Participants

In this trial, Robin Ursa, Kim Doyle, and Jo Deer have names that are gender neutral; therefore, these individuals may be either male or female.

Plaintiff: Attorneys, Goldie Locks, Cpl. Kim Doyle, Buford Bear

Defense: Attorneys, Jo Deer, Beulah Bear, Robin Ursa

Formulating Questions for Direct and Cross-Examination

The mock trials in this book have been designed to allow for no clear-cut solutions. It is up to the attorneys to explore the affidavits of the opposition for weaknesses and inconsistencies. It is very important that all affidavits be looked at in this way, so that students can prepare for cross-examination. Students should be especially careful to analyze the affidavit of each witness to determine what information is fact or opinion. *Opinions are only admissible as testimony if offered by an expert witness.* An example would be a DNA expert who could give an opinion as to whether physical evidence at a crime scene matched the DNA pattern of a person accused of the crime.

I have found it best to allow the students to explore their own ideas first. Then, ask them specific questions and have them suggest possible ways that both the prosecution and defense might approach each question. By doing this, the students come to understand that they must look at all aspects of the case from both sides. The sample question below gives possible approaches by the prosecution and the defense.

Example: Why didn't Goldie Locks say something about Buford Bear's visit to her office when she was apprehended?

Prosecution: She was startled and frightened. She had just awakened and was not thinking clearly.

Defense: She realized she had trespassed and shouldn't have been in the house.

GUMPERVILLE GAZETTE

Gumperville's Neighborhood Newspaper

May 12, Volume 8, No. 82

Local Realtor Arrested for Breaking and Entering

by Fran Statler, Gazette Reporter

Goldie Locks, a local real estate agent specializing in rental properties, was taken into custody by Gumperville Police this morning. She was reported to have entered the home of Buford and Beulah Bear at 864 Forest Parkway when they were not at home. Gumperville Police received two 911 calls alerting them that someone was in the home without the Bear family being present. One call came from Beulah Bear and the other from a neighbor.

When police officer Cpl. Kim Doyle, entered the home, a room-by-room search was begun. Having been alerted by a neighbor that the intruder was probably in a bedroom, the officer found the realtor asleep in one of the beds. The officer woke her up. She identified herself as Goldie Locks and denied entering the house without permission. She said she was there at the request of Buford Bear. When asked if this was true, Beulah Bear said she was sure her husband would have told her if he had asked a strange blonde to enter their house when no one was home. Robin Ursa, a neighbor of the Bears who placed the other 911 call, agreed with Mrs. Bear and commented, "You can be sure I will keep my doors locked from now on. There are all kinds of disreputable characters moving into town."

Officer Doyle took the suspect into custody and drove her to the police station for booking.

Desk sergeant L.A. Briggs said that Gumperville is usually a peaceful place and that the last time they had put someone in jail was back in 1998 when Darius Dudley had been arrested for disorderly conduct. This celebrated story was in the news for weeks.

Dudley had damaged mailboxes and trash cans when he had an argument with Rufus Monahan over ownership of a stray pig. The disagreement took a turn for the worse when Dudley discovered that Monahan had invited guests over for barbecued ribs and pork chops and had not invited Dudley.

Dudley paid for replacement of the mailboxes and trash cans, but the two have never revived their once-friendly relationship.

Sergeant Briggs stated that it was hoped that Locks, who had moved to Gumperville recently, had not damaged the town's bucolic image.

NOTE: This story was late-breaking and filed close to the time the *Gazette* goes to print; therefore, it was impossible to include photos. **SEE TOMORROW'S ISSUE FOR EXCLUSIVE PHOTOS OF THE APPREHENSION OF THE PERPETRATOR.** Also featured will be details of an investigation into a possible criminal background of the accused, Goldie Locks.

Figure 7. Copy of Gumperville Gazette's front-page story on Goldie Locks.

GUMPERVILLE SOCIAL NEWS

THIS WEEK'S EVENTS

Today, 2 p.m.—Ladies Garden Club at Lula Deering's house on Appletree Circle. Bring cuttings of your favorite flowers or seeds from last year's garden. Cookies and punch will be served.

Thursday, 8 p.m.—Monthly meeting of the Bruins' Club. Swearing in of new officers. Be sure to wear your Club fez. Refreshments will be served. Bruins' Hall.

Friday, 3 p.m.—Afternoon meeting of Gumperville Scouts, immediately after school. All Cub Scouts are asked to wear their uniforms. This is the monthly "Show and Tell" meeting, so scouts are asked to bring an interesting leaf, plant, or rock found in and around the woods of Gumperville. Plans for the annual father/ cub camping trip will be discussed.

Friday, 6 p.m.—Potluck dinner, Gumperville Civic Center. Bring your favorite salad, soup, main course, or dessert to share with your neighbors. Coffee, tea, and soft drinks will be served.

Saturday—Planning meeting for Memorial Day Celebration. Any group planning to march in the parade must have its application in at this meeting.

DOOLEY'S GARDEN CENTER

Come to Dooley's for the largest selection of flowers, potting soil, mulches.
Come to Dooley's for the largest selection of tools, planters, and pots
Come to Dooley's for the best prices in Gumperville
Come to Dooley's for a
Beautiful Garden.

WE STRIVE FOR ACCURACY!

Local real estate agent, Goldie Locks, has been released from custody by the Gumperville Police Department. A story in the Gazette *on May 12 reporting that she had trespassed at the home of Buford and Beulah Bear at 864 Forest Parkway, Gumperville, proved to be incorrect. The Gumperville Gazette regrets the error.*

Figure 8. Copy of *Gumperville Gazette's* page 23 retraction story on Goldie Locks.

You may want to use some of the following questions as guidelines in helping students prepare direct and cross-examination. (Remind the students that an attorney never asks a question on cross-examination unless he or she knows the answer the witness will give.)

- Why didn't Buford Bear help Goldie Locks to get a retraction in the paper when it wasn't in soon after the event?
- Why didn't Jo Deer check out the story about Goldie Locks with the police before putting an article in the *Gazette*?
- Does Robin Ursa always go around looking into people's windows?
- How can the front door being slightly open, as Goldie Locks claims, be explained?
- Does Goldie Locks always go into people's houses and walk around if no one is at home?
- Why didn't Cpl. Doyle call for back-up?
- Why is Beulah Bear willing to testify on behalf of Jo Deer?

Trial Documents

The pages that follow include a statement of facts about the trial, affidavits from each witness, and forms for the jury to record a verdict. These forms are reproducible and should be given to all students helping to prepare for the trial. You may also wish to make copies of the two newspaper pages available.

IN THE COUNTY COURT OF THE
THIRD JUDICIAL CIRCUIT, IN AND
FOR FITZWILLY COUNTY, _____

GOLDIE LOCKS
Plaintiff
v.

JO DEER, Owner and Editor of the *Gumperville Gazette*
Defendant

STATEMENT OF FACTS

At 7:38 a.m., on May 12, the Gumperville Police Department received a call from Robin Ursa of 834 Forest Parkway. The caller stated that there was an unknown vehicle parked in the rear of the home of Buford and Beulah Bear, neighbors of the caller. The caller stated that the Bears did not have a car and they usually went for a morning walk, so it was doubtful they were home.

At 7:42 a.m., on May 12, the Gumperville Police Department received a 911 call from the cell phone of Beulah Bear. She, her husband, Buford, and child, Buttons, had gone for their morning walk. During the walk, the elder Bears had argued and Mrs. Bear and Buttons had returned home without Mr. Bear. Upon approaching the house, she found the front door of their home at 864 Forest Parkway slightly open. She stated that she had closed the door when they had gone for their morning walk in the wooded area near their home. She asked that a patrol car be sent over to investigate.

At 7:45 a.m., Sgt. L.A. Briggs of the Gumperville Police dispatched a patrol car to the scene. Cpl. Kim Doyle was the investigating officer. At the same time, reporter Fran Statler of the *Gumperville Gazette* heard the event on a police scanner and drove to the scene.

Cpl. Doyle entered the Bear resident, gun drawn, and proceeded to search the residence. The officer heard snoring and upon further investigation found a woman asleep in one of the bedrooms. Upon awakening her and questioning her, it was ascertained that her name was Goldie Locks and she did not live in the house and had entered it when no one was home. The officer asked Mrs. Bear if she recognized the individual and she said she did not. After reading the suspect her rights, Cpl. Doyle placed her under arrest.

As they were leaving the house, the newspaper reporter, who had been outside talking to Robin Ursa, took pictures of Ms. Locks in handcuffs as she got in the patrol car. Cpl. Doyle drove the suspect to headquarters for booking and Fran Statler returned to the *Gazette* offices to file a story about the break-in that was later printed on the front page of the afternoon edition of the *Gumperville Gazette*.

At around 10 a.m., Buford Bear returned home. Not wanting to go right home after arguing with his wife, he had stopped at the barn of a friend, Sal Grizzly, to admire his new Jack Stag riding lawn mower. Upon his arrival, Mr. Bear's wife, Beulah, told him what had happened. She described the woman who had been apprehended and Buford saw the car parked at the rear of the house. Recognizing the car, he explained to Beulah that the car belonged to Goldie Locks, a new real estate agent in town who specialized in rental properties. Because the Bears were planning to open their bed-and-breakfast soon, he thought Ms. Locks might be able to help. He thought she would be coming over later in the day. He also admitted that he had forgotten to lock the door when they left for their walk.

After Buford explained this to the police, Ms. Locks was released. Unfortunately, the afternoon edition of the *Gazette* had gone to press and was delivered before anyone realized that the charges were false. The story occupied a prominent spot on the front page with headlines. When the editor, Jo Deer, realized the error, a retraction was printed in the May 17 issue. It appeared on page 23 and was brief.

Ms. Locks is charging that her reputation had been damaged and that it has cost her in commissions earned from her real estate business. She wants restitution for damage to her reputation and a retraction on the front page of the *Gazette*. In addition, Ms. Locks would like to be given possession of any negatives and prints of the photos taken and a written order issued to stop publication or distribution of said photos.

IN THE COUNTY COURT OF THE
THIRD JUDICIAL CIRCUIT, IN AND
FOR FITZWILLY COUNTY, _____

GOLDIE LOCKS
Plaintiff
-v-
JO DEER, Owner and Editor of the *Gumperville Gazette*
Defendant

GENERAL AFFIDAVIT

<u>Goldie Locks</u>, being first duly sworn according to law, deposes and says that:

My name is Goldie Locks. I moved to Gumperville a few months ago. I had originally lived in a large city and wanted to experience a community that was quiet and friendly. I had worked for a large real estate firm before and thought that I could use my experience to open my own office here in town. I planned to specialize in rentals, because many of the people here hibernate during the winter months and only use their homes part of the year.

I had barely put up a sign in the window of my small office when Buford Bear walked in. He said he and his wife, Beulah, had hoped to open a small bed-and-breakfast inn in their home. They would manage it themselves most of the year, but would have competent help to run it when they hibernated. The one thing he was anxious about was getting someone to screen possible guests because they would be sharing his home. He asked if I could possibly do that. I said I could do quick background checks for him. He requested that I come over and see his home, which they planned to call Beulah and Buford's Bed-and-Breakfast. I said I would, but that I would call first.

I have a severe problem with insomnia. I rarely get more than 2 hours of sleep each night. On the morning of May 12, I got up around 6 a.m. I had been awake most of the night. Rather than just sit around the house, I decided to go for a drive. I thought it might be a good idea to just drive past the Bears' house because I had never seen it. I had not planned to stop, but it was so cozy and charming. I noticed that there was evidence suggesting that people in the house were up. Blinds were open and the front door was slightly ajar. A doormat had written on it "Mi Casa es su Casa" (My home is your home). How inviting! I thought. I rang the doorbell and knocked on the door. No one answered. I entered the house, calling out. This was a mistake. Once inside, I saw a charming home, just perfect for a bed-and-breakfast inn. The kitchen was homey. There were even wicker baskets containing varieties of instant oatmeal set out on the table. What was even more thoughtful was that the bowls were of different sizes to accommodate different sized appetites. Throughout the house, this special treatment was evident. There were rocking chairs of different sizes to accommodate guests of varying weights. As I entered the bedrooms, I noticed the beds were special, too. One bed had a very tailored appearance. I sat on it and it was very firm. Another bed had a soft and fluffy comforter. I sat on it and sank way down. It was definitely too soft. The third bed had an attractive spread in my favorite shade of blue. I sat down on it and it felt wonderful—so good that I decided to give it a real test and lie down. I was so exhausted that I must have fallen asleep almost immediately.

Suddenly, I awoke and found a police officer standing over me. I was asked my name and whether or not I lived in this house. I said I did not. Mrs. Bear then entered. She said she did not know who I was and she had never seen me before.

I was read my rights, placed under arrest, and escorted to the police cruiser. As I came out of the house, a camera flashed and an individual, who I later learned was a reporter for the *Gumperville Gazette*, asked me questions. There were other people standing around, but frankly, I was so upset, I couldn't tell you who they were.

Several hours after I was taken into custody to the police station, Buford Bear came in and told the police that he had requested that I look at the Bears' house and it was all a misunderstanding. I was released from custody.

That afternoon, as I stopped by my office, I saw a newspaper stand with the *Gazette* on it. The front-page headline read, "Local Realtor Arrested for Breaking and Entering." The article went on to say that I had entered the Bears' house through an unlocked door and had been found sleeping in one of the bedrooms. It stated that Mrs. Bear was very upset that a stranger had entered their home. There was no picture attached to the article.

I went to the *Gazette* office and demanded a retraction. The editor, Jo Deer, apologized profusely and said there would be retraction in the very next issue. Several days passed and then on May 17, I found a retraction on page 23. It was just a few sentences.

Since the incident I have had no business and people look at me as if I am a common criminal. It is embarrassing. In addition, I would like to know what happened to the pictures that were taken.

I request that the *Gumperville Gazette*, its publisher and editor, be made to pay an amount to make restitution for income lost and damage to my reputation. In addition, I would like to have any negatives and prints of the photos taken and an order be issued to stop publishing or distribution of said photos.

_____
Affiant

SWORN TO AND SUBSCRIBED before me this _____ day of

_____ , in the year _____

_____
NOTARY PUBLIC

State of _____

My Commission Expires: _____

GOLDIE LOCKS
 Plaintiff
-v-
JO DEER, Owner and Editor of the *Gumperville Gazette*
 Defendant

GENERAL AFFIDAVIT

<u>Cpl. Kim Doyle, Gumperville Police</u>, being first duly sworn according to law, deposes and says that:

My name is Cpl. Kim Doyle. I have been with the Gumperville Police for almost 10 years and was promoted to the rank of Corporal 6 months ago.

On the morning of May 12 at 7:45 a.m., I received a call from headquarters that there had been a possible break-in at the Bears' home on Forest Parkway. When Sgt. Briggs said they had two calls, I knew it had to be serious. When I arrived at the scene, Robin Ursa and Beulah Bear were standing in front of the house. Robin told me that the front door of the house was open. Knowing that the Bears usually took a walk in the morning and always closed the door, Robin made a call. Now, it is not unusual to get a call from Robin. Robin phones in about once or twice a month—usually nothing serious. When I saw Beulah Bear and she said she also had made a call, I knew that this might be the scene of a crime.

I drew my gun (it doesn't have any bullets in it, but criminals don't know that) and stealthily advanced into the house, checking each room. Having already looked in all the windows, Robin was able to warn me that a blonde woman was asleep in one of the beds. Still, you can't be too careful. I went into each room and finally, there she was! Just as Robin said, she was fast asleep and snoring.

I knew I had to be careful. You never know. Some of the most vicious criminals in history have been women who looked helpless and innocent. I gently tapped her on the shoulder and she awoke with a start. I also knew I had to follow the guidelines in the Gumperville Police Manual. I asked her name. I had seen her around town, but I didn't know who she was. She replied, "Goldie Locks." I asked her if she lived in the house (I knew she didn't, but you've got to follow procedure). She said she didn't. She said that she had been invited by Buford Bear to look over the house. The Bears were possibly thinking of starting a bed-and-breakfast. This sounded like it might be a good explanation, but just to be safe, I asked Beulah (Bear). She was very upset and said she knew nothing about it. She verified that they were thinking of starting a bed-and-breakfast but was sure her husband, Buford, would have told her if he had contacted any real estate agent about it. She said the thought of anyone walking into a house uninvited was unbelievable. She then saw that Ms. Locks had a couple of packets of the Bears' brand of special oatmeal sticking out of her handbag. "Look," she cried, "she's a thief, too."

I pondered the situation. I saw Fran Statler of the *Gumperville Gazette* outside listening and taking pictures. I knew how awful it would look if I didn't take her down to the stationhouse if she was really guilty of some terrible crime. Can you imagine seeing the pictures in the paper and the headlines reading "Gumperville Police Corporal Let Known Criminal Go"? I couldn't take the chance. I read her rights to her and took her to the station so we could do a background check for a possible criminal record. Sgt. Briggs booked her on charges of trespassing and burglary and took the oatmeal packets as evidence.

A little after 10:30 a.m., Buford Bear came in and verified Ms. Locks' story. He said there was no problem with her taking the oatmeal packets as he had told her to do a thorough evaluation of their home as a possible bed-and-breakfast. She was just doing her job. She was released from custody. I felt bad for her, but if I had to do it all over again, I would. You can't be too careful these days.

_____
Affiant

SWORN TO AND SUBSCRIBED before me this _____day of _____, in the year _____

_____
NOTARY PUBLIC

State of _____

My Commission Expires: _____

IN THE COUNTY COURT OF THE
THIRD JUDICIAL CIRCUIT, IN AND
FOR FITZWILLY COUNTY, _____

GOLDIE LOCKS
 Plaintiff
-v-
JO DEER, Owner and Editor of the *Gumperville Gazette*
 Defendant

GENERAL AFFIDAVIT

<u>Buford Bear</u>, being first duly sworn according to law, deposes and says that:

My name is Buford Bear and I live at 864 Forest Parkway, Gumperville, with my wife Beulah and our daughter, Buttons. We have lived there ever since Beulah and I were married 10 years ago.

A few weeks ago, Beulah and I had a discussion about finances. Berry picking hasn't been as profitable as it once was and we needed to look for other sources of income. We looked at our home and thought we had come up with the perfect solution. Our home is large with several bedrooms, most of which we do not use. We have a nice large kitchen with a big table and plenty of chairs. We thought we might look into setting up a bed-and-breakfast. We came up with the name "Beulah and Buford's Bed-and-Breakfast"—thought it sounded kind of homey. We planned to run it ourselves part of the year and then hire someone to live here and run it while we were away on hibernation. Beulah was worried about how we could be sure to have good guests, and more importantly, a good manager to take over when we were not here. We also wanted the image of the bed-and-breakfast to be consistent, so Beulah developed her own instant oatmeal. This way, even if we weren't there, the food would taste consistently good.

About a week ago, I was walking through town and saw there was a new real estate office. The name on the window was "Goldie Locks Realty." Underneath it said, "Specializing in Real Estate Rentals." I thought this might be a good place to inquire about our plans. When I went to the office, Goldie Locks greeted me with a friendly smile and asked me to sit down. She agreed I couldn't be too careful when having someone share our home, whether it be as a guest or a manager in our absence. She said if we hired her, she would screen potential managers, as well as guests. Her fee seemed reasonable. She said before she could draw up a contract, she would need to see our house. I told her any time would be fine. She said she would call first.

On May 12, Beulah, Buttons, and I went for our usual morning walk. We left the house around 6:30 a.m. I mentioned to Beulah that our old lawn mower was not working well, and that we should really look into getting a new one, perhaps a riding one. She appeared to be agreeing when we rounded the bend to Sal Grizzly's place and saw him outside on his Jack Stag riding mower. It was a thing of beauty. Beulah saw it and immediately got in a huff. She said I merely wanted to keep up with the Grizzlys and our present lawn mower was just fine. When I tried to reason with her, she left with Buttons in tow. I really didn't want to go home with her so angry, so I stopped to talk to Sal. He offered me a cup of coffee and we began to talk. You know, just ordinary stuff. Before I knew it, it was almost 10 o'clock.

I hurried home and found Beulah in a real huff, sitting at the kitchen table with our neighbor, Robin Ursa. Now, there's a real busybody. I looked outside and saw the car and asked if Goldie Locks was there. Beulah told me that Ms. Locks had entered the house when we were not home and they found her sound asleep in Buttons' bed. Then she told me the police had been called and Ms. Locks was arrested. Beulah said that in addition to trespassing, Ms. Locks had stolen several packets of our oatmeal.

I explained that it was all a mistake and that I had invited her to come to the house at any time to discuss the bed-and-breakfast idea and possibly make some suggestions about how we could have our idea work well. Unfortunately, I had forgotten to tell Beulah this, which made her all the more furious. I can't help it. I tend to forget things and had not thought to mention this to Beulah.

At any rate, I went down to the police station and explained the situation and they released Ms. Locks. I explained to her what had happened and she said she understood and that she really should have called first.

Everything seemed to be reconciled, until the afternoon issue of the *Gumperville Gazette* hit the stands. I saw the headlines and knew that Ms. Locks had been treated unfairly. I thought they would surely have a retraction on the front page the following day, but I never did see one. Sal Grizzly told me it had been printed about a week later and it was just a few sentences and way in the back of the paper. Ms. Locks has a right to be angry. She was trying to set up a new business in town and now her reputation is damaged.

If I've learned one thing from this whole mess, it's that I have got to remember to tell Beulah about important events in our lives. Right now, I'm trying to figure a way to tell her that I ordered a Jack Stag Supermower the day before this all happened. Maybe I'll go into hibernation early this year.

_____
                                                             Affiant

SWORN TO AND SUBSCRIBED before me this _____day of _____, in the year _____

_____
                                                NOTARY PUBLIC
State of _____

My Commission Expires: _____

IN THE COUNTY COURT OF THE
THIRD JUDICIAL CIRCUIT, IN AND
FOR FITZWILLY COUNTY, _____

GOLDIE LOCKS
Plaintiff
-v-
JO DEER, Owner and Editor of the *Gumperville Gazette*
Defendant

GENERAL AFFIDAVIT

<u>Jo Deer</u>, being first duly sworn according to law, deposes and says that:

My name is Jo Deer and I have been editor and owner of the *Gumperville Gazette* for about 6 years. I bought the paper from Sammy Gumper. Mr. Gumper was a member of the family for which Gumperville was named, and he founded the newspaper. He had tried for years to sell the paper but had trouble finding a buyer. I had been an English teacher in Darbytown for many years and thought that running a small town newspaper would be an ideal retirement activity. My family still lives in Darbytown. We have lived there all of our lives so we didn't want to move.

I commute about an hour each day, arriving at the office around 5 a.m. The paper is usually "put to bed" at around 11 a.m. and then printed and distributed late in the afternoon. This allows our carriers (mostly teenagers) to deliver the paper after school. After the paper goes to the printer, we immediately start setting up the paper for the following day. Items that are not time-sensitive can be set up at this time. We found that most people like to have an afternoon newspaper because they usually are too busy in the morning to read a paper.

The one drawback about living so far away is that I really don't get to know the people of Gumperville. I knew of the Bear family and from what I could tell they were really nice folks. I had not met or even seen Goldie Locks before this event. I had passed her office on the way to work, but frankly, I rarely go out of the office to drive around town. Being editor of a small-town newspaper is a full-time job.

When Fran Statler came in with the story, I'll admit I was excited that we had a "real" story to put on the front page. This town is rather quiet and not too much that is "newsworthy" happens around here. For example, the week before this happened, our main story was about the gopher problem at the Mills' house. So, you can see when we had a reported "trespassing" and "burglary" here in our little town, this was big news. I decided not to wait for the pictures to be developed. We could put them in the next day's paper. I wanted to get the story out before our local "vocal reporter," Robin Ursa, got on the telephone to get the word out. Robin likes to share the latest news with others as quickly as possible.

The paper had been printed and delivered when I got a phone call from Goldie Locks. She was very upset. She explained the situation and the fact that she had been exonerated. She demanded a retraction and wanted the negatives of the pictures. I told her I would put a retraction in the paper, but that the photos were the property of the newspaper. I called the police station and spoke to Sgt. Briggs. He confirmed her story.

To tell the truth, the next day, a Friday, was a pretty busy one. In addition, to the newspaper, I had promised to do a lecture on journalism at the school where I used to teach. I really couldn't get out of doing it. When I finally got into the office to do the paper, everything was rushed because I got a late start. The paper only comes out Monday through Friday. There are no Saturday or Sunday editions. The following Tuesday morning, Goldie Locks came storming into my office. She wanted to know what had happened to the retraction. It was the first time I had actually met her. I told her it had slipped my mind and I would get the retraction in the paper in that day's edition. It was near the time for the paper to go to the printer. It was actually all set with only a little space on the Social page. I debated whether to wait until the next day and do a bigger story, but then realized I had promised her to put the retraction in that day and I like to keep my word.

I don't see how she can say she has lost commissions from not having any business. She hasn't been here that long and people I've spoken to said they had never heard of her until the newspaper article. Seems to me this was pretty good publicity for her. As for the photos, we promise not to print them, but they *are* the property of the *Gumperville Gazette*.

_____

Affiant

SWORN TO AND SUBSCRIBED before me this _____ day of _____, in the year _____

_____

NOTARY PUBLIC

State of _____

My Commission Expires: _____

IN THE COUNTY COURT OF THE
THIRD JUDICIAL CIRCUIT, IN AND
FOR FITZWILLY COUNTY, _____

GOLDIE LOCKS
 Plaintiff
-v-
JO DEER, Owner and Editor of the *Gumperville Gazette*
 Defendant

GENERAL AFFIDAVIT

<u>Beulah Bear</u>, being first duly sworn according to law, deposes and says that:

My name is Beulah Bear and I live at 864 Forest Parkway, Gumperville, with my husband, Buford and our daughter, Buttons. This is my dream house and I have decorated it in the latest country furnishings. It's very roomy and really charming, if I do say so myself.

The only problem is that the upkeep on the house has been rather expensive. Buford's berry picking business has not been doing well and because this is only a seasonal job, we have no money coming in during the winter months. This is usually not a problem because we do go into hibernation at that time. We discussed how we could earn more income. I looked around the house and saw we had a couple of extra rooms that we really didn't use. We also had a large and spacious eat-in kitchen. I had seen something like this in *Forest Housekeeping* (you know, the magazine for forest homes). They showed a rabbit couple who had turned their warren into a bed-and-breakfast for other hares. I thought, "Why can't we do something like this for other bruins?"

The question then arose about what would happen when we were away. I suggested hiring some one to "mind the store." Buford said he thought it was a good idea but wondered how we could find someone reputable to do this. He said he would look into it. That was the last I'd heard of it.

On May 12, the three of us went for our morning walk. Buford suggested we take a different way home "just for a change." As we turned a bend in the road, I knew why he wanted to take this route. There was that Sal Grizzly sitting atop his new riding mower. When I saw the look in Buford's eye, I knew he really wanted one. He always has to have the latest tools and gadgets. A trip to Forest Depot with him is a nightmare. I knew we couldn't afford a new mower, but he said we would be able to with the new income that would be coming in from the bed-and-breakfast. He was spending money we didn't even have. We argued and I took Buttons by the hand and went home.

As I got near the house, something did not look right and I saw the front door was open. I was sure I had closed it when I left. I saw a car parked nearby. To be safe, I called 911. I spoke to Sgt. Briggs who said a car would be sent right out.

It turns that Robin Ursa, our neighbor, also had called. What a relief to have such a caring neighbor!

Cpl. Doyle of the Gumperville Police arrived in just a few minutes. It turns out that because two 911 calls were made the situation was given "priority" status. Cpl. Doyle entered the house, gun drawn. I waited outside, not wanting to get caught in any crossfire. After what seemed like an eternity, the police officer brought this blonde woman out. I was asked if I knew who she was. I said I had never seen her before. She just stood there in a daze. The officer read her rights to her, handcuffed her and helped her into the car. All the while this was happening, this person, I guess a reporter for the *Gazette*, was snapping pictures and talking to Robin.

I really wished that Buford had been there. Suppose I had gone into the house without calling 911 and found this woman asleep in the bed. Who knows what she might have done? I was unarmed and defenseless.

Around 10 o'clock, Buford *finally* arrived home. As soon as he saw the car, he asked where Goldie Locks was. I told him what had happened and he explained that he had asked her to stop by the house. He hadn't expected her this morning because she said she would call first. He ran out of the house down to the police station and explained everything to Sgt. Briggs. Goldie Locks was released. Unfortunately, the editor of the *Gazette* wasn't aware of this. To them, this was a major story. Because the reporter had arrived back in the office so close to the deadline, the paper went to print. Fortunately, there were no photos because there was not enough time to get them ready for printing.

When Goldie Locks saw the article on the front page of the paper, I heard she was very angry. She demanded a retraction and wanted the pictures, too.

I really can't blame Jo Deer—an editor has to do whatever is necessary to get the news out to the public in a timely manner.

_____

Affiant

SWORN TO AND SUBSCRIBED before me this _____day of _____, in the year _____

_____

NOTARY PUBLIC

State of _____

My Commission Expires: _____

GOLDIE LOCKS
 Plaintiff
-v-
JO DEER, Owner and Editor of the *Gumperville Gazette*
 Defendant

GENERAL AFFIDAVIT

<u>Robin Ursa</u>, being first duly sworn according to law, deposes and says that:

My name is Robin Ursa and I live at 830 Forest Parkway, Gumperville—that's right next to Beulah and Buford Bear. I've known them since before they were married and moved here—a really nice couple. Their daughter, Buttons, is a very sweet little girl.

A few weeks ago, Beulah Bear mentioned that she and Buford were considering turning their home into a bed-and-breakfast. I know the financial situation is a bit tight in their house so I guess they thought this might be a solution. At that time, I voiced to Beulah my concerns over having strangers staying in her home overnight when the Bears were home and even worse, having a manager care for it when they went on hibernation. Who would watch over the goings on while no one was here? (I tend to go on hibernation at around the same time.)

At any rate on the morning of May 12, I looked out my front window and saw a strange car parked in front of the house. I knew the Bears were not home, as they go for their morning walk around 6:30 a.m.—rain or shine. I walked to the front of the house and saw the front door wide open. I assumed the Bears had come home to welcome the visitor. I walked around the house, peeking in the windows. The Bears were nowhere in sight and while the table had been set for breakfast, the oatmeal packets were still unopened and the milk had not been taken out of the refrigerator.

When I got to one of the small bedrooms, there she was! This blonde woman was lying on one of the beds, fast asleep and snoring away. I didn't know her name, but I had seen her walking around town recently and eating at Black Bear's Diner. She was very distant and never said "hello" or anything.

Well, I felt it was better to be safe than sorry, so I went home and called 911 and spoke to Sgt. Briggs at the police station. He said he would send a car over to investigate. Apparently, at around the same time, Beulah had arrived home and called 911 on her cell phone when she saw the front door was open. When the police cruiser pulled up, I told Cpl. Doyle where I had seen this woman sleeping. Cpl. Doyle went into the house, gun drawn.

Meanwhile, Fran Statler from the *Gumperville Gazette* arrived. I told the reporter what had happened. We waited until Cpl. Doyle came out of the house with Ms. Locks handcuffed. Apparently, Fran had gone back to the car and now had a camera. Judging from the amount of flashes going off, I would say that at least a dozen pictures were taken.

Ms. Locks and Buford Bear say that it was a mistake and she was not trespassing. At the time Ms. Locks was arrested, no one knew that the two had prearranged this meeting—certainly not Beulah. If we are going to err in such a case, it is better to do so on the side of caution. No one knew when the paper went to press that her visit had been prearranged. This was unfortunate, but it is more important that the newspaper let the citizens know of any possible dangers. Suppose she had been a real criminal? Then, the *Gazette* would have been praised for its role in the incident. Jo Deer did apologize in the paper. What more could you ask for?

_____
Affiant

SWORN TO AND SUBSCRIBED before me this _____ day of _____ , in the year _____

_____
NOTARY PUBLIC
State of _____

My Commission Expires: _____

IN THE COUNTY COURT OF THE
THIRD JUDICIAL CIRCUIT, IN AND
FOR FITZWILLY COUNTY, _____

GOLDIE LOCKS
Plaintiff
-v-
JO DEER, Owner and Editor of the *Gumperville Gazette*
Defendant

JURY BALLOT

VERDICT

Please circle your choice (YES or NO)

Jo Deer, Owner and Editor of the *Gumperville Gazette*, shall be held responsible for damage to Goldie Locks' reputation because of an article published in the *Gumperville Gazette* and shall be ordered to pay damages.

YES   NO

If you voted YES, list the amount between $1 and $10,000.00 that Jo Deer should have to pay _____

Jo Deer shall be ordered to give the following to *Goldie Locks.*

All existing prints of photos taken by reporter Fran Statler of Goldie Locks on May 12.

YES   NO

All existing negatives of photos taken by reporter Fran Statler of Goldie Locks on May 12.

YES   NO

DATED in Gumperville, Fitzwilly County, _____, this _____ day of _____, _____

_____
Foreperson

Squanto Jones v. Myles Standish

Background Information

When the Pilgrims came to America from England in 1620, they landed on the shores of what is now Rhode Island and Massachusetts. This was territory inhabited by the Wampanoags, part of the Algonkian-speaking peoples. The Wampanoags treated nature and each other with respect. Any visitor to their home shared whatever food they had, even if there was little. The Native Americans extended this same courtesy when they met the Pilgrims.

One of the Wampanoags was named Squanto, who had been to England with an explorer named John Weymouth. There, Squanto learned to speak English. While in England, he also met Samoset, of the neighboring Wabanake Tribe, who also had gone to England with an explorer. Upon their return to America, they discovered that everyone in the Patuxet village had died. They went to a neighboring village to stay.

The following spring, Squanto and Somerset were hunting and came upon their deserted village and saw a group of people living there. These were the Pilgrims who had come the year before. Half of them had died and the remaining ones were in poor condition. Squanto and Samoset decided to stay with them for a few months to teach them how to survive in their new home. They taught them how to hunt, how to grow corn and other vegetables, how to build native-style homes, and generally how to survive using the native environment. By fall, the Pilgrims were able to live on their own and survive the winter with stored foods and shelter.

Captain Myles Standish was the leader of the English group. He had learned that the Algonkian tribes traditionally held six thanksgiving feasts a year. To show his gratitude, he invited Squanto, Samoset, and other members of the Wampanoags for a thanksgiving feast. The Pilgrims had no idea how large the tribe was and were ill prepared for the arrival of about 90 relatives of Squanto and Samoset. Massasoit, the leader of the Wampanoags, sent some of his men home to bring food. Thus, the natives supplied most of the food for the first feast, which lasted 3 days. There was a peace and friendship agreement between the two groups that gave the Pilgrims the clearing in the forest where the Patuxet village once stood. This became the new town of Plymouth.

More English people came and they benefited from the knowledge learned by the first pilgrims. Religious differences soon surfaced between the Pilgrims and the natives. The relationship between them deteriorated and within a few years, the children of both groups were fighting each other in what came to be known as King Phillip's War.

For the mock trial, I have taken the story of the early settlers and the Wampanoags and updated it to modern times. Myles Standish is the leader of a group that has come to New England thinking they can live as they once did back in England. Members of the group were farmers and they believed they could grow the same crops here. Unfortunately, this was not so. Again, the Native Americans, Squanto Jones and Samoset Smith come to their rescue. Squanto Jones owns a restaurant called Wampanoags' Restaurant. As in the original story, the Pilgrims are treated to a Thanksgiving feast. When they realize the dire straits that the newcomers are in, Squanto and his group teach them how to farm the land and make the most of natural resources. The two groups see each other from time to time, but there is little social interaction between them.

In time, the newcomers forget about the generosity of their benefactors. They open a competing restaurant, Pilgrim's Fare. The recipes are remarkably similar to those served at Wampanoags' Restaurant. At first, Squanto Jones is merely upset, but when his restaurant starts losing money, he realizes he must take legal action. He has decided to sue Myles Standish and Pilgrim's Fare, charging him with stealing trade secrets. A modern-day war between the two factions has begun.

Definitions

t/a—trading as.

Trade secret—An idea that is novel and different whose owner is entitled to protect it from exploitation by others. Secret recipes that have been developed for a product are the personal property of a company. Basically, a trade secret is information including a formula, pattern, compilation, program, device, method, technique, or process that is confidential. It is not common knowledge but it is not protected by a patent. The most common violation of a trade secret occurs when an employee goes to another company. An employee who leaves the company and uses the secret recipe to establish his or her own business has taken property from his or her former employer. Although the corporation never patented or copyrighted the secret recipe, it still has a property right in the idea. To protect a trade secret, the business must make reasonable effort to maintain secrecy. If you have an idea that is valuable, the people to whom you disclose it must sign a confidentiality agreement, or you will lose ownership.

Exhibits

- Confidentiality Agreement for Wampanoags' Restaurant (see Figure 9)
- Menu for Wampanoags' Restaurant (see Figure 10)
- Menu for Pilgrim's Fare Restaurant (see Figure 11)

Trial Participants

In this trial, Darby Chandler, Terry Fleming, and Jamie Doright have names that may be used for either male or female witnesses.

Plaintiff: Attorneys, Squanto Jones, Samoset Smith, Darby Chandler
Defense: Attorneys, Myles Standish, Terry Fleming, Jamie Doright

Formulating Questions for Direct and Cross-Examination

The mock trials in this book have been designed to allow for no clear-cut solutions. It is up to the attorneys to explore the affidavits of the opposition for weaknesses and inconsistencies. It is very important that all affidavits be looked at in this way, so that students can prepare for cross-examination. Students should be especially careful to analyze the affidavit of each witness to determine what information is factual and which is opinion. *Opinions are only admissible as testimony if offered by an expert witness.* An example would be a DNA expert who could give an opinion as to whether physical evidence at a crime scene matched the DNA pattern of a person accused of the crime.

I have found it best to allow the students to explore their own ideas first. Then, ask them specific questions and have them suggest possible ways that both the prosecution and defense might approach each question. By doing this, the students come to understand that they must look at all aspects of the case from both sides. The sample question below gives possible approaches by the prosecution and the defense.

> *Example:* Why did Squanto and the other members of his group freely show Myles Standish and the other newcomers how to prepare the special foods?
> *Plaintiff:* They realized the newcomers were in dire straits and wanted to help them. They thought the recipes would be used for their own use only.
> *Defense:* They had no reason not to share them. The recipes were common knowledge to any cooks in the area.

You may want to use some of the following questions as guidelines in helping students prepare direct and cross-examination. (Remind the students that an attorney never asks a question on cross-examination unless he or she knows the answer the witness will give.)

- Why would Squanto Jones have employees sign an agreement not to reveal recipes if he did not believe they were "trade secrets" and special recipes?
- Why didn't Myles Standish and his group try something new and different in their restaurant rather than something so similar to Wampanoags'?
- Why did Terry Fleming go to work at Wampanoags'?
- Why is the mayor testifying on behalf of Myles Standish?

- Why did it take so long for Squanto Jones and his group to realize that Myles Standish was building a restaurant?
- What are some reasons that Squanto Jones has not renovated his restaurant?

Trial Documents

The pages that follow include a statement of facts about the trial, affidavits from each witness, and forms for the jury to record a verdict. These forms are reproducible and should be given to all students helping to prepare for the trial. You also may wish to make copies of the Confidentiality Agreement (Figure 9) and the two restaurant menus (Figures 10 and 11) available to them.

Confidentiality Agreement

I, Squanto Jones t/a Wampanoags' Restaurant certify that items listed on the menu of the above restaurant are original and distinctive. These foods have been prepared solely for distribution to our customers at the restaurant.

These items include foods listed under the Soup, Entree, Side Dish, and Dessert categories of the menu. A dated copy of said menu is attached to this agreement. Recipes for such foods are to be treated as "trade secrets."

The undersigned, an employee of Wampanoags' Restaurant, agrees that by signing this agreement, he/she shall not divulge these recipes to anyone while he/she is employed at Wampanoags' or at any time after he/she has left the employment of said restaurant.

_____   _____
Squanto Jones   Date
t/a
Wampanoags' Restaurant

_____   _____
Employee   Date

Figure 9. Wampanoags' Restaurant employee confidentiality agreement.

Wampanoags' Restaurant
Authentic Native American Fine Dining

SOUPS
- Wild mushroom
- Cream of turkey
- Corn soup
- Fish chowder

ENTREES (*according to availability*)
- Roast turkey with herbed stuffing
- Baked salmon with savory sauce
- Roast pheasant with chestnut dressing
- Stewed rabbit with wild onion gravy
- Roast venison with baked apples

SIDE DISHES
- Baked squash (with buttery topping)
- Corn on the cob (grilled in the husk)
- Green beans Squanto (an original chef's recipe)
- Baked potato (baked in our brick ovens)

DESSERTS
- Homemade pumpkin pie (with our special flaky crust)
- Homemade apple pie (with special spices)
- Corn pudding (a Wampanoag favorite)

Dinner $14.95
Includes choice of soup, entree, two side dishes, dessert, and cornbread.
Beverages are not included.

Choice of beverages: Coffee, tea, or apple cider—$1.25

PLEASE NOTE: All food served at Wampanoags' is from game hunted in our local forests, fish caught in our local streams, or from our own fields of home grown vegetables and fruits.

Figure 10. Wampanoags' Restaurant menu.

Pilgrim's Fare

Serving your favorite local cuisine with an English flare

A full four-course meal for only $14.49 (Including beverage)

SOUPS

Turkey noodle soup
Corn chowder
Cream of mushroom
New England Clam Chowder

ENTREES

Hasenpfeffer (stewed rabbit)
Grilled salmon with lemon parsley marinade
Roast wild turkey with chestnut stuffing
Pheasant with apples
Venison pot roast with sour cream sauce

SIDE DISHES (*Choose two*)

Savory squash casserole
Grilled corn on the cob
Green beans simmered with a special herb mixture
Potatoes (baked in the skin or mashed)

DESSERTS

Homemade pies :
    Apple, Pumpkin, or Berry
Corn pudding (with a special caramel sauce)

Meals include tea or coffee. Cider or lemonade—$1.50

Figure 11. Pilgrim's Fare menu.

IN THE CIRCUIT COURT OF THE
SECOND JUDICIAL CIRCUIT, IN AND FOR
PLYMOUTH COUNTY, MASSACHUSETTS

CASE NO: 88-321-CA

SQUANTO JONES t/a Wampanoags' Restaurant
    Plaintiff

-v-

CAPTAIN MYLES STANDISH t/a Pilgrims' Fare
    Defendant

STATEMENT OF FACTS

Two years ago, Squanto Jones t/a Wampanoags' Restaurant had had an exceptionally good year and wanted to share his good fortune with his neighbors. On Thanksgiving Day, instead of opening his business to regular customers, he decided to share a feast with those less fortunate than him. A large group of people had recently moved into the area from England and, apparently, they were not aware of ways to make ends meet. He thought that if he invited them to a complimentary dinner, he might also be able to make arrangements to show them how to grow their own food and use local wildlife for sustenance.

The restaurant was extremely popular because all of the items on the menu were home grown or from local wildlife. Venison, turkey, pheasant, fish, pumpkin, corn, potatoes, berries, and many of the other foods served all were native to the area's land and lakes.

Mr. Jones sent an employee, Samoset Smith, to the home of Captain Myles Standish who appeared to be the group's leader. He readily accepted the invitation.

At around noon on Thanksgiving Day, the group arrived. Squanto Jones decided to have much of the food prepared beforehand so that members of his staff could join in the celebration. Because hunting had been particularly successful, turkey was the meat chosen for the entree. Corn, squash, corn soup, cornbread, beans, and pumpkin and apple pies completed the menu.

The feast lasted for hours and there was a great deal of discussion about how the newcomers could learn from the natives about how to survive and feed their families simply by using the resources at hand. The natives agreed to help them whenever possible. Everyone seemed to have a wonderful time. If any of the guests wished to take leftovers home with them, they were provided with containers.

Squanto Jones and his group worked with the newcomers group regularly to show them how to grow their food and hunt for wildlife and edible berries and plants in the area. They also showed the newcomers how to prepare the food as it was done in the restaurant. After a few months, they felt that their work was done and Captain Standish and his group had learned all they needed to know about using the land and wildlife to survive. The following Thanksgiving, Captain Standish's group invited the Native Americans to share a feast with them. Squanto Jones was amazed at how well they had learned to prepare the foods. They had duplicated the recipes they had been shown. The two groups lived peacefully but rarely socialized after that. The following spring, a building was erected down the road from Wampanoags' Restaurant. It wasn't until a few days before it was to open that Squanto Jones realized that the newcomers were opening their own restaurant, Pilgrim's Fare. At first, Jones felt that the two restaurants would coexist and maybe bring more traffic into the area. He sent Samoset Smith to the restaurant to investigate the situation. A plant was offered as a goodwill gesture for success in the restaurant. Samoset brought a menu from the restaurant back with him. It was almost identical to the fare served at Wampanoags' Restaurant.

When Pilgrim's Fare opened 5 months ago, crowds came to eat at the new restaurant and business decreased at Wampanoags' Restaurant. In fact, they lost many of their loyal customers.

Squanto Jones has brought suit against Captain Myles Standish, stating that he and his group have not acted in good faith, that the recipes given to them were for the group's personal use and not for a commercial venture. He further states that the similarity in the menus of the two restaurants has left no doubt that Standish has stolen recipes that could be regarded as trade secrets.

Squanto Jones is asking for monetary damages for lost business and that an order be issued stopping the Pilgrim's Fare from serving items similar to the signature soups, entrees, side dishes, and desserts served at Wampanoags' Restaurant.

That winter was very hard for us, but with the help of the Wampanoag group, we survived. We were able to hunt and fish and gathered berries and edible plants from the forest. In the spring, we planted our first crop. Although we made some mistakes, things grew fairly well for us. That fall, we decided to reciprocate and invited Squanto Jones and his employees to a feast. We didn't have a large building like the restaurant, so we had the feast outside.

Wanting to show how much we had learned, we prepared many of the same dishes that they had served us the previous Thanksgiving. At first, Squanto didn't seem too pleased, but then congratulated us on how well the feast had turned out.

After that, we didn't really associate with the Native Americans. You might say that they had their culture and we had ours. Oh, we were friendly if we met them on the street, but we really didn't socialize with them.

A couple of years passed and our group was getting by much easier than when we first came to America. The men were doing odd jobs and the women also were finding sources of income. We were pooling our money and before long, we had a substantial amount saved. At one of our group's meetings, someone suggested that we might do even better if we started our own business venture. Several types of businesses were discussed and then someone suggested that we open a restaurant. This was met with some disfavor. Some said that we had never done anything like this before, but then someone said we could model it after Wampanoags' Restaurant. The comment was made that there were several fast food chains that were similar and they all succeeded. We had several excellent cooks who could take care of the kitchen, and several of our members had a business background. After many meetings, we decided to build a restaurant that had a real English feeling to it. We would use the game, fish, and locally grown crops like Wampanoags' served. This certainly would make it more cost effective.

The restaurant, Pilgrims' Fare, had a very successful opening. We thought that the crowds would diminish after the newness of the restaurant wore off, but we were wrong. In fact, there were more customers. Word had spread. There were few restaurants in this area and people apparently were tired of going to Wampanoags' Restaurant. In addition, we had added a little flare to some of the basic recipes and our restaurant was new, whereas Wampanoags' was badly in need of some fresh paint.

We don't feel like we stole anything from Wampanoags' Restaurant. There are only so many different kinds of game in the area and only so many ways of preparing them. This area is big enough to accommodate two restaurants and if the food and service is good and the atmosphere friendly, both should do well.

_____

Affiant

SWORN TO AND SUBSCRIBED before me this _____ day of _____ in this year _____

_____

NOTARY PUBLIC
State of Massachusetts

My Commission Expires: _____

CASE NO: 88-321-CA

SQUANTO JONES t/a Wampanoags' Restaurant
    Plaintiff

-v-

CAPTAIN MYLES STANDISH t/a Pilgrims' Fare
    Defendant

GENERAL AFFIDAVIT

Terry Fleming, being first duly sworn according to law, deposes and says that:

I was one of the original group members who came to America with Captain Standish several years ago. He is quite a leader. Most of us were doing very poorly back in Lancashire, England. He gave us hope and organized us into a group that worked well together.

When we first came to America, we all wondered if we had made a mistake. Things were very difficult, and we lost some of our group members to illness. The turning point was when the Native Americans helped us. They showed us how to hunt, fish, and grow crops. I'll never forget that first Thanksgiving when they showed us hospitality, and we realized we too could survive by using what nature had to offer. We really had no idea how to prepare the foods available, but when we tasted what they had cooked for us at that feast, it was really an eye opener. I had worked in a pub in England doing some cooking, what you call here "short order cooking." You couldn't say I was a chef, but I did know the basics about cooking a meal.

The year after we had that first Thanksgiving feast was an eventful one. We learned so much from Squanto and Samoset and their group. They showed us how to hunt and fish and what plants growing naturally were edible as vegetables or fruits or for seasoning.

They were incredibly generous. The abandoned houses we found in the woods used to be theirs. When they built new homes closer to town, they rarely returned to these houses, using them only for weekends or vacations. When they found we had settled there, they let us stay, saying they really didn't need them and we could keep using them as long as necessary.

The following Thanksgiving, I suggested to Captain Standish that we invite the newcomers for a feast of our making. In this way, we could show our appreciation and show them how well we had learned the lessons they had taught us. Many of the dishes were the same as they had served us the year before. Some of our women had taken notes on the leftovers from the first feast and observed how they were prepared. I believe that, in some cases, they improved on the original.

Conditions continued to improve for us. We all are hard workers. In fact, I believe that people who leave their country for a new land are motivated and will work hard. We also were a very tight knit group and we all became U.S. citizens at the same time. We kept pretty much to ourselves and pooled our savings. Many of us worked odd jobs.

I even worked at Wampanoags' as an assistant cook in the kitchen. I really got some insight into how they prepared their food. When I went to work there, I signed some sort of paper. I felt it was just a formality and I didn't really read it. Now, Squanto Jones says it was a "Confidentiality Agreement."

When someone suggested that we start a new business, I recommended that we open our own restaurant. There was a lot of resistance to the idea. Few of our group had worked in a restaurant or anything like one. After many, many discussions, we agreed that our group had several good cooks and several who had business experience. All of us had one thing in common—we were willing to work hard.

The thought of patterning our restaurant after Wampanoags' met with much resistance in the group. Some felt that we would do better to offer a different type of fare—fish and chips or something of a fast food variety. Others felt that we should offer the types of food we prepared on a daily basis. We knew how to do this and because we had community meals and often cooked for a large group, this was much like cooking for a restaurant.

We all worked hard building the restaurant (some of our members had construction experience), and we had a very successful opening. We had far more customers than we had anticipated. Word spread and people did not mind waiting for a table. We thought that it was the novelty of a new restaurant, but months have gone by and business is better than ever.

I admit our menu is similar to Wampanoags' menu, but I would think they would be flattered. Hasn't it been said "imitation is the sincerest form of flattery"? This is what is great about America—free enterprise. Wampanoags' needs to reinvent itself, spruce up the place and do a bit of advertising. There is plenty of business for two well-run restaurants in this area.

_____

                                                                  Affiant

SWORN TO AND SUBSCRIBED before me this _____ day of
_____ in this year _____

_____

                                                  NOTARY PUBLIC
                                                  State of Massachusetts

                                                  My Commission Expires: _____

CASE NO: 88-321-CA

SQUANTO JONES t/a Wampanoags' Restaurant
    Plaintiff

-v-

CAPTAIN MYLES STANDISH t/a Pilgrims' Fare
    Defendant

GENERAL AFFIDAVIT

<u>Jamie Doright,</u> being first duly sworn according to law, deposes and says that:

I've been mayor of this town for almost 9 years—I was just elected to my third term last November. Since I've been mayor, our town has grown in many ways, which is displayed by the increase in our population and number of businesses.

When Captain Standish and his group first moved here, I'll admit that most people were a bit wary. They were foreigners and the group was different from the local folk. At first, they stayed at a local inn, but within a short time they moved into the Wampanoag tribe's old place. I heard some of them became ill and didn't survive. I doubt that anyone else would have helped them if it hadn't been for Squanto Jones and his group. That first Thanksgiving when he had them over to his restaurant was a real turning point. Just goes to show what fine people we have living in these parts. Apparently the help was what the foreigners needed. They were quick learners and hard workers.

I've known Squanto since we both were children. We went to the same school. Our families didn't socialize much—not much in common, I guess. His restaurant has been the most popular place around, mostly because there weren't any other really good restaurants near here—only fast food places. The menu hasn't changed in years and the place looks much like it did when we were kids.

When Captain Standish came into the town hall for a permit to build his restaurant, we were all surprised. His plan was well thought out and it soon became the buzz of the town that there was going to be another restaurant. People were really excited. I can't believe that no one at Wampanoags' knew about it until shortly before its opening. In the few years since they moved here, the English people have really tried to become part of the community. They were active in several of our community organizations—why, they even campaigned for me in the last election.

I've eaten at Wampanoags' many times, of course, and now I frequent Pilgrim's Fare. The menus are alike and the food appears to be prepared in a similar manner at both places. We are fortunate to have two fine restaurants serving excellent cuisine. The main difference is the ambiance. Wampanoags' has the same familiar, homey atmosphere it has had for many years. Pilgrim's Fare is fresh and new. If the food is equally good in both restaurants, people are going to go to the one that looks the freshest. As for Squanto's claim that they have stolen his trade secret recipes, I really don't think it is fair to say that. The recipes are merely words written on paper. The ingredients may be the same but the techniques used to prepare the food can make a big difference.

_____

Affiant

SWORN TO AND SUBSCRIBED before me this _____ day of
_____ in this year_____

_____

NOTARY PUBLIC
State of Massachusetts

My Commission Expires: _____

IN THE CIRCUIT COURT OF THE
SECOND JUDICIAL CIRCUIT, IN AND FOR
PLYMOUTH COUNTY, MASSACHUSETTS

CASE NO: 88-321-CA

SQUANTO JONES t/a Wampanoags' Restaurant
    Plaintiff
-v-
CAPTAIN MYLES STANDISH t/a Pilgrims' Fare
    Defendant

JURY BALLOT

VERDICT
Please circle your choice.

Captain Myles Standish, t/a Pilgrim's Fare, has not acted in good faith, by using recipes that had been given for the group's personal use for a commercial venture. These recipes are to be regarded as trade secrets.

        YES   NO

Captain Myles Standish, t/a Pilgrim's Fare, shall be ordered to cease serving items similar to the signature soups, entrees, side dishes, and desserts served at Wampanoags' Restaurant. The defendant shall also be ordered to discontinue using the menu similar to that presented at Wampanoags' Restaurant in style and items offered.

        YES   NO

Captain Myles Standish, t/a Pilgrim's Fare, shall be ordered to pay to *Squanto Jones,* t/a Wampanoags' Restaurant, damages for lost business as a result of the use by Pilgrim's Fare Restaurant of recipes regarded as trade secrets.

        YES   NO

If the jury has voted YES, list the amount between $1 and $30,000.00 that *Captain Miles Standish,* t/a Pilgrim's Fare Restaurant, shall pay for lost business.

Amount for lost business $_____

        DATED in Plymouth County, Massachusetts, this ____day of _____
                               in the year_____

                               _____
                               Foreperson

Appendix: Glossary of Legal Terms

abolition: abolishing or ending slavery.

acquittal: action taken by a jury when, upon trial, they find that the accused is not guilty and enter a verdict accordingly.

affidavit: a written statement sworn to before an officer who has authority to administer an oath.

civil disobedience: refusal to obey government's demands or commands in a nonviolent manner.

contempt of court: any willful disobedience to, or disregard of, a court order or any misconduct in the presence of a court; punishable by fine, imprisonment, or both.

defendant: the person defending or denying; the party against whom relief or recovery is sought in action or suit or the accused in a criminal case.

evidence: all facts, testimony, and documents presented for the purpose of proving or disproving a question under inquiry.

felony: a serious crime, such as murder, larceny, or robbery, punishable by death or by imprisonment in a state or federal penitentiary.

grand jury: at common law, a group of persons consisting of not less than 12, nor more than 24, who listen to evidence and determine whether or not they should charge the accused with the commission of a crime by returning an indictment. The number of members on a grand jury varies in different states.

habeas corpus: an order signed by a judge directing a sheriff or other official, who has a person in his custody, to bring that person before the court to determine whether or not he should be released from custody.

hearsay: evidence that is not entirely within the personal knowledge of the witness but is partly within the personal knowledge of another person.

indictment: a formal written charge against a person presented by a grand jury to the court in which the jury has been sworn.

judgment: the declaration, by a court, of the rights and duties of the parties to a lawsuit that has been submitted to it for decision.

misdemeanor: a crime (less serious than a felony) punishable by fine or imprisonment in a city or county jail rather than in a penitentiary.

notary public: an official authorized by the state to attest or certify legal documents.

perjury: the offense of willfully making a false statement when one is under oath to tell the truth.

preponderance of evidence: evidence of greater weight or more convincing than the evidence that is offered in opposition to it; that is, evidence that as a whole shows that the fact sought to be proved is more probable than not. With respect to burden of proof in civil actions, it means evidence that is more credible and convincing to the mind.

plaintiff: the party who complains or sues in a civil action and is so named on the record; a person who seeks remedial relief for an injury to rights.

prosecution: a proceeding instituted and carried on by due course of law before a competent tribunal for the purpose of determining the guilt or innocence of a person charged with crime; the continuous following up, through instrumentalities created by law, of a person accused of a public offense with a steady and fixed purpose of reaching a judicial determination of the guilt or innocence of the accused.

reasonable doubt: reasonable doubt that will justify acquittal is doubt based on reason and arising from evidence or lack of evidence, and doubt that a reasonable man or woman might entertain. It is not fanciful doubt, is not imagined doubt, and is not doubt that a juror might conjure up to avoid performing an unpleasant task or duty.

subpoena: an order directed to an individual commanding him or her to appear in court on a certain day to testify in a pending lawsuit.

suffrage: the right of voting.

trade secret: An idea that is novel and different whose owner is entitled to protect it from exploitation by others. Secret recipes that have been developed for a product are the personal property of a company. Basically, a trade secret is information including a formula, pattern, compilation, program, device, method, technique, or process that is confidential. It is not common knowledge, but it is not protected by a patent.

venue: the county in which the facts are alleged to have occurred and in which the trial will be held.

verdict: the decision made by a jury and reported to the court on matters lawfully submitted to them in the course of the trial of a case.

About the Author

Betty M. See has had a varied teaching career. She taught seventh- and eighth-grade language arts, was a middle school classroom teacher, and for 10 years she worked with gifted students in grades 3–8. At each of these levels, she often used simulation activities to help students become involved in the learning process.

When working with gifted students, mock trials were one of her students' favorite activities. At first, Betty obtained the materials for these trials from the local bar association. Unfortunately, the subject matter was not always appropriate for students at this level. As a result, she wrote trials using characters familiar to the students. These trials were the basis for her successful first book, *Jury Trials in the Classroom.*

In *More Jury Trials in the Classroom,* she has created additional trials. As with the first book, the participants are familiar and an element of humor has been added to further pique the interest of the students.

Betty is a teacher who has retired from the classroom, but has never given up her love of teaching and writing. She and her husband, Bob, retired to Florida and live at an airpark, the Leeward Air Ranch, in Ocala, FL, where he flies his Piper Archer and she is editor of the community newsletter, *Happy Landings.* In addition to editing, she regularly submits humorous columns about aviation and life in general.

IN THE CIRCUIT COURT OF THE
SECOND JUDICIAL CIRCUIT, IN AND FOR
PLYMOUTH COUNTY, MASSACHUSETTS

CASE NO: 88-321-CA

SQUANTO JONES t/a Wampanoags' Restaurant
    Plaintiff

-v-

CAPTAIN MYLES STANDISH t/a Pilgrims' Fare
    Defendant

GENERAL AFFIDAVIT

<u>Squanto Jones</u>, being first duly sworn according to law, deposes and says that:
My family has lived in this area for generations. We can trace our heritage back to before any settlers came from Europe. We have always welcomed newcomers and helped them in any way we can. We believe that everyone should help his fellow man.

My grandfather opened Wampanoags' Restaurant about 50 years ago. He named it after the tribe to which our family belongs. He was looking for a business that could be a family venture and could help spread the word of our Native American culture. All of the food prepared and served was made with ingredients hunted in our forests, caught in our local streams, or grown locally. We take pride in excellent service and a menu that reflects our heritage. My grandfather passed the running of the restaurant down to my father who, in turn, passed it onto me. I have been owner and manager for more than 10 years.

Four years ago, in the spring, a large group of people came to this area. Word soon spread that they had come from England. They moved into a settlement that our family had once lived in, but now used rarely except for a weekend get-away now and then. The houses were really primitive and afforded the bare minimum of shelter from the elements. Some people called them squatters, but it was apparent they were in need and knew little about living in these parts. We felt they needed the houses more than we did, so we let them stay.

We occasionally ran into some of them and we could tell from their appearance that they were not doing well. Their clothes had become ragged and hung on them because they were so ill fed.

In early fall, our staff, most of whom are from the Wampanoag tribe, discussed the upcoming holiday season and how we would decorate the restaurant. It has always been our tradition to close Wampanoags' on Thanksgiving Day and Christmas to allow our staff time to spend these holidays with their families. Someone mentioned that the newcomers were not doing well and wondered how they would survive the harsh winters that we have in these parts. They apparently had some farming skills, but did not know about local crops. They had brought wheat seed from England but it would not grow in this area. Then our head chef,

Samoset Smith, suggested that we might open the restaurant on Thanksgiving Day for the newcomers only. The staff could all bring their families and we would share the holiday in a true meaning of Thanksgiving.

Samoset went to Captain Standish's house and extended an invitation to him and the members of his group. He readily accepted.

On Thanksgiving Day, Captain Standish and his group of about 30 people arrived. The staff of our restaurant had prepared a feast that included many of the standard items on our menu. Because we are used to serving large groups, it was really not any more work than an ordinary day. What made it different was that our families shared the food with newcomers to our area who were in need. This is something our people believe in doing—helping those who are less fortunate.

Captain Standish and several members of his group seemed very interested in the foods we had served and asked how they were prepared. Samoset and several of the cooks in the kitchen gave them general directions but were not specific about the exact ingredients and preparation methods. After all, our recipes were original and our staff knew that to share them with others was to reveal our "trade secrets." In fact, when our cooks are hired, they agree that the recipes are not to be shared either while they are employed by us or if they leave and work for someone else. Our group did, however, offer to show Captain Standish and his group where they could hunt and fish as we did. Because the newcomers seemed to be destitute, it was the only right thing to do. We also told them how they could prepare their land for a spring planting and how they could find berries and edible plants in the woods. Not only were they given advice that day, we continued to help them in the following months.

The following year, Captain Standish invited our group to a Thanksgiving feast. They did not have a large enough room to accommodate everyone, so we sat outside on picnic tables. The food served was well prepared. In fact, many of the dishes were prepared exactly as we had shown them. I was astonished, but happy that they were doing so well.

While we shared these two feasts, there was actually little contact between the two groups. In the late summer of last year, Samoset and I noticed that a new building was going up about 2 miles down the road. This area is growing, so we at first paid no attention.

Then we saw the sign going up announcing "Pilgrim's Fare Restaurant." Samoset was upset, but I told him this might bring more people to the area and our restaurant might profit too. He agreed and he went to Pilgrim's Fare and brought a potted plant as a goodwill gesture. When he came back, he was very upset. He had a copy of their menu. The items on it were essentially the same as what we served at Wampanoags' Restaurant. They also offered a four-course dinner at a fixed price like we did. I mentioned this to Captain Standish and he said that the food served was nothing unusual and there were other restaurants that served the same recipes. This was common fare in this part of the country.

We know for a fact that this is not so. We have customers who drive many miles because our food is so unusual and so well prepared.

In the beginning, Pilgrim's Fare had huge crowds, as might be expected with a new restaurant opening. We expected it to taper off, but it didn't. We lost many of our regular customers.

We believe that Captain Standish and his group violated our right to maintain trade secrets. Our recipes are unique, and we do not give them out even if a customer asks for them. When we showed the newcomers how to prepare the foods, it was because we wanted to help them. We never expected them to take this knowledge and open their own restaurant. They have violated a trust by using our trade secrets for their own benefit.

As a result, we have had a noticeable loss of revenue from our business. We ask that they change their menu and stop serving foods that are similar to those served at Wampanoags' Restaurant. We further ask for compensation for the business lost. We have tried to be good neighbors, but apparently Captain Standish and his group do not know the meaning of living in harmony.

_____

Affiant

SWORN TO AND SUBSCRIBED before me this _____ day of _____ in this year_____

_____

NOTARY PUBLIC
State of Massachusetts

My Commission Expires: _____

IN THE CIRCUIT COURT OF THE
SECOND JUDICIAL CIRCUIT, IN AND FOR
PLYMOUTH COUNTY, MASSACHUSETTS

CASE NO: 88-321-CA

SQUANTO JONES t/a Wampanoags' Restaurant
   Plaintiff
-v-
CAPTAIN MYLES STANDISH t/a Pilgrims' Fare
   Defendant

GENERAL AFFIDAVIT

<u>Samoset Smith</u>, being first duly sworn according to law, deposes and says that:

Squanto Jones and I are cousins. Our grandfather founded Wampanoags' Restaurant and our fathers worked together there also. It has always been a family-owned restaurant and Squanto and I carried on the tradition. Because he is older, he is the manager of the restaurant. He knows every last detail about the operation of Wampanoags' from ordering supplies to the preparation of all of our signature dishes. Everyone regards him as the boss.

I guess you might say I am the head chef. It is my job to make sure that the customers get their meals prepared exactly as they request. We have some people who have been coming here for years, as did their parents before them. We almost consider them to be family.

From early on, members of the Wampanoag tribe instill in their children that it is our obligation to help others—especially those in need. When we saw the sorry state that the newcomers were in when they first arrived from England, we had no choice but to help them. They are our fellow man. The Thanksgiving feast that we shared with them their first year here was memorable. They were so appreciative and were eager to learn how to live in this area, which apparently was different from their English home. They asked about the foods we served and how they were prepared. Squanto and I discussed what we could do to help them. We agreed that there was enough game and fish in the forest for all of us and that we should show them how to hunt and fish. Squanto said we could give them basic instructions on how certain foods could be prepared—you know baked, broiled, or roasted, but we would draw the line at the "secret recipes" we used at Wampanoags.' Our restaurant is, or shall I say, was different from anything in the entire Northeast. We have had many people tell us this. We had a reputation and we had to protect it.

We hired a couple of the newcomers to help in the kitchen. One of them, Terry Fleming, had some experience in England as a cook and mastered the preparation of many of our entrees. He worked here for about a year and then left saying he wanted to try another line of work. After that, I didn't talk to him so I had no idea about the plans for their new restaurant. What he was actually doing was working here as a spy. The fact that so many of the dishes at Pilgrim's Fare are like ours is proof of that.

Some say we should have been aware that the new restaurant was being built. Frankly, we spend so much time working that we have little time to read the local papers, so we were not aware of the restaurant's existence until it was completed and nearly ready for opening. Actually, it wouldn't have made any difference. We expected it to be a different kind of restaurant. We never expected Pilgrim's Fare be an imitation of Wampanoags' Restaurant.

We have lost a lot of business since they have opened, however, we have lost much more than just business. We have lost faith in our fellow man. We helped them in their time of need. We did not expect that they would turn on us and threaten our very livelihood.

I think that the novelty of Pilgrim's Fare will wear off and people will see it for what it is—a shabby imitation of a local institution. We have been told that we should redecorate and give our place a new look. It is our custom to paint or stain the natural woods we have inside the restaurant every 2 years. The floors are made of natural wood and washed daily. We want Wampanoags' to reflect the natural look of our Native American heritage. It may not have a new modern look, but if it did, it wouldn't be Wampanoags' Restaurant.

_____
Affiant

SWORN TO AND SUBSCRIBED before me this _____ day of
_____ in this year_____

_____
NOTARY PUBLIC
State of Massachusetts

My Commission Expires: _____

CASE NO: 88-321-CA

SQUANTO JONES t/a Wampanoags' Restaurant
    Plaintiff
-v-
CAPTAIN MYLES STANDISH t/a Pilgrims' Fare
    Defendant

GENERAL AFFIDAVIT

Darby Chandler, being first duly sworn according to law, deposes and says that:

I am a local resident of Plymouth County, MA. For the last few years, I have written a food column for the local newspaper, the *Wampanoag Press*. Previously, I served in the U.S. Navy as a cook aboard several different ships. One of them was an aircraft carrier. I traveled to many different countries and have eaten at many restaurants around the world. I am familiar with all types of cuisine. When I came home on leave, I always looked forward to coming to Wampanoags' Restaurant for one of their famous Native American dinners. From my experience, it ranks as a world-class restaurant. The following is an excerpt from a column I wrote last year about Wampanoags':

> I've had pheasant in France that can't compare with the roasted pheasant that Wampanoags' serves. There is something unique in the seasoning that is hard to duplicate. The stewed rabbit is another example of a culinary delight. This is a delicacy in Germany, but they can't hold a candle to the way the dish is made at Wampanoags'. The flavor is delicate without being overpowering. Venison is another entree that can be tricky. If not prepared properly, it can taste very gamey. I must say that turkey is not served much elsewhere in the world. If they ever decide they want to learn how to prepare it in Europe, I would tell them to ask Squanto how to do it properly.
>
> Cooks sometimes have difficulty with side dishes. They tend to overdo the presentation. Simple is better. From the grilled corn, to the squash and green beans at Wampanoags', they are all delectable. And, what Wampanoags' does with a baked potato is difficult to imitate. I guess the stone ovens must be the secret.
>
> As for desserts and soups, Wampanoags' has chefs that specialize only in each of these areas. The results are outstanding.

Not only is the food delicious, the price is right too. All meals are price fixed at $14.95 with children under 12 dining for $6.95. Servings are ample and everyone is sure to take home a carry-out container.

This describes how I feel about Wampanoags' Restaurant. I know that Squanto Jones is very protective about his recipes. They have been handed down for generations and are definitely unique. When Standish's Pilgrim's Fare opened, I was delighted to see another restaurant. People enjoy eating out and this area can definitely support two fine restaurants. When I went to dine there the first time, I was surprised and disappointed to see that the menu was essentially the same as Wampanoags' menu. I cannot understand why they didn't try to do something different. To virtually duplicate Wampanoags' offerings seemed ill advised.

_____

Affiant

SWORN TO AND SUBSCRIBED before me this _____ day of
_____ in this year _____

_____

NOTARY PUBLIC
State of Massachusetts

My Commission Expires: _____

IN THE CIRCUIT COURT OF THE
SECOND JUDICIAL CIRCUIT, IN AND FOR
PLYMOUTH COUNTY, MASSACHUSETTS

CASE NO: 88-321-CA

SQUANTO JONES t/a Wampanoags' Restaurant
    Plaintiff
-v-
CAPTAIN MYLES STANDISH t/a Pilgrims' Fare
    Defendant

GENERAL AFFIDAVIT

<u>Myles Standish</u>, being first duly sworn according to law, deposes and says that:

I immigrated from Lancashire, England, about 5 years ago with members of my family and community. There were many reasons for leaving—many of us did not have jobs and we were looked down upon by those who were not of the same faith. Our group had members who had many different skills, and we thought we would be able to settle in America and create our own new community. Unfortunately, things did not go as we had planned. We thought we would find jobs here and be able to have suitable housing. We came in the early spring, planning to start some wheat crops on land that we could perhaps lease. We though that the wheat, plus whatever we could manage to gather by hunting and fishing, would sustain us.

We came upon an abandoned community deep in the woods near a lake. Although the houses were in a rather rundown condition, they did provide us with shelter. Some members of our group worried about how we would fare during the cold winter months, especially because our wheat crop had not fared well. Apparently, wheat that will grow in England is not suitable in American soil. We lost some of our members from illness.

One day in early November, we received a visit from one of the Native Americans—Samoset Smith. Samoset extended an invitation from Squanto Jones, the owner of Wampanoags' Restaurant. Our entire community was invited to a Thanksgiving Day dinner at the restaurant. Of course, we accepted. It came at a time when we were sorely in need of friends and a decent meal.

The restaurant was closed for the day and all of the employees and their families joined us. The food was wonderful. We had never tasted many of the dishes and, of course, asked how they were made. Squanto was reluctant to tell us at first, but said that his group would show us how to find the ingredients for the dishes. What particularly interested us was that all of the food was from the forests, lakes, and lands nearby. Squanto and his group were most generous. Over the next few months, they helped us learn where to hunt and fish and in the spring, taught us how to plant crops that would grow well in this area.

Perhaps I didn't mention it, but when we had that first Thanksgiving dinner, we had many leftovers to take home. Some of our women are very good cooks. They had observed what they could by watching some of the food preparation. When we brought the food home, they sat and tasted it and took notes about what they thought the ingredients were and how they were prepared.